Science and Morality in Medicine

Science and Morality in Medicine

a survey of medical educators

Earl R. Babbie

UNIVERSITY OF CALIFORNIA PRESS

Berkeley, Los Angeles, London 1970

University of California Press
  Berkeley and Los Angeles, California

University of California Press, Ltd.
  London, England

  Copyright © 1970, by The Regents of the
  University of California

Library of Congress Catalog Card Number: 71–92674
  SBN: 520–01559–2

  Printed in the United States of America

To my father
Herman O. Babbie
and his physician and friend
Anthony Piro, M.D.

Contents

Foreword

The triumphant progress of medical technological insight and manipulation is currently producing in its wake two sets of major problems relating to optimal medical care in general. One revolves around the adequate distribution and availability of such care; the other around the danger of becoming infatuated with the technological aspects of the medical approach, that is, of ceasing to question its limitations. Speaking more concretely, this means unintentionally losing sight of the axiomatic foundations of medicine—man cannot be understood only in mechanical terms. And this, in turn, invites the possibility of unintentionally violating these foundations.

Dr. Babbie has devoted his sociological skills to the clarification of this second set of problems. His study should benefit everyone, patient and physician alike, but especially those concerned with recognizing and teaching the axiomatic foundations of medicine at the present time.

The problem of the awareness of the axiomatic foundations of medicine and the danger of becoming infatuated with the technological approach obviously revolves around the double aspect that man's nature basically presents: the person/thing dualism. The answer to the question is obvious too. In the words of the great Spanish medical historian Lain Entralgo: "Medicine has always been, and always had to be in one way or another 'psychosomatic,' " [1] and, one may add: has to be, unless one wants to ignore that most basic experience in being ill, the disease/dis-ease dualism, and wishes to delegate the primary obligation of taking care of the sick to some specialists. The recognition of this primary issue of medical care does not mean, of course, that specialization is an evil aspect of medical development or medical education; it definitely is not. It means that those responsible for medical education must be vigilant about providing in their institutions a pivotal place for attending to the problem of this dualism.

The concept of "the" physician and his methodology has interested me for quite some time.[2] It was my good fortune to be able to interest Professor Charles Y. Glock, at that time director of the Survey Research Center at the University of California at Berkeley, and, through him, Dr. Earl R. Babbie in these problems. Dr. Babbie then undertook the very tedious and exacting task of polling the core group of medical educators on their attitudes toward their primary obligation and on their actual activities. It is this particular undertaking which he presents here and for whose execution we are indebted to him; no empirical/statistical study equals the one in hand.

As is apparent from reading this book, Dr. Babbie even

1. Pedro Lain Entralgo, *Mind and Body, Psychosomatic Pathology: A Short History of the Evolution of Medical Thought,* trans., Aurelio M. Espinosa, Jr. New York: P. J. Kenedy & Sons, 1956.
2. E.g., "On Defining Medicine," *The Christian Scholar,* 46 (1963): 200–211, and "Medical Humanism: A Redundant Phrase," *The Pharos of Alpha Omega Alpha,* 32 (1969): 12–15.

transcends his original task and explores some strictly sociological problems in relation to the medical attitudes of the educators who were polled. But this part of the work is outside my field of competence.

Obviously the most difficult theoretical problem of an undertaking like this survey is to formulate questions precise enough to allow only a single interpretation. From this point of view—and Dr. Babbie agrees—a clear differentiation between fellowship with someone and responsibility in the sense of partnership on the one hand, and care of something and responsibility in the sense of an engineer's responsibility for the optimal functioning of a machine on the other is especially difficult. In a future iteration of the survey this problem, it seems to me, needs particular attention. As I remarked in the beginning, herein lies, for me, the greatest value of Dr. Babbie's book. In it we have both a point of reference from which we can very concretely increase our characterization of the timeless responsibilities of the primary physician, and a baseline against which we can measure historically the actual performances of medical schools in relation to these responsibilities.

Otto E. Guttentag, m.d.
San Francisco Medical Center
University of California

Preface

This is a study of science and morality in contemporary American medicine. It grows out of an initial concern for the frequent allegations that scientific emphases have progressively dehumanized medical practice in this country by undermining the traditional norms of humane patient-physician relations. Beginning with this initial concern, the work progresses, ultimately, to a consideration of very general issues of social and medical morality.

Typically, the blame for dehumanization in medicine has been laid at the door of the nation's medical colleges. It is suggested that medical school faculty members have become so engaged by the marvels of science that they have ceased to care about human beings and have, consequently, ceased to train humane physicians. Unaccountably, these allegations have never been the subject of empirical testing, despite their undeniable significance for the future of medicine.

In 1963, Professor Otto E. Guttentag of the San Francisco Medical Center engaged the support of the National Institute of Health for a national survey of medical school faculty members—"Medical Research and Clinical Responsibilities" (Grant #GM09981). The purpose of the survey was to examine, empirically, the impact of medical science on medical morality. This book is a result of that survey.

While the issues raised in this book are by no means limited to medical school faculty members, there are good reasons for examining this group before turning to a consideration of the medical profession as a whole. First, teaching physicians are among the most esteemed physicians in the nation. With regard to medical innovations, they are not only where the action is, they *are* the action. Their orientations and activities, therefore, have a disproportionately strong influence across the medical profession.

At the same time, they possess the power and bear the responsibility for training the future physicians of the nation. If medical science does indeed weaken faculty members' commitments to humane medicine, this effect is likely to radiate from them, horizontally across the present profession and vertically across the new generations of physicians.

Finally, a study of the interplay between science and humane care of patients should be conducted under circumstances which permit an examination of both quantities. In this respect, a survey of medical school faculty members is especially appropriate. More than practicing physicians in the community, these teaching physicians have close and continuing contacts with medical research, either through participation or through association. At the same time, faculty members, in the clinical departments at least, are closely involved in patient care within the university. In view of their intimate contacts with both patient care and medical science, medical school faculty members would seem to be most meaningful subjects for an initial examination of medical science and medical morality.

What follows is an analysis of data collected in the national survey of full-time faculty members in the clinical departments of Medicine and Pediatrics at twelve of the nation's medical colleges. The data were collected during the 1965–66 academic year.

The book is divided into three parts, representing the chronological development of the analysis. Since each part is built upon the findings of the preceding ones, it is difficult to introduce each of them at this point without first presenting all the major findings. Therefore, each part of the book is introduced separately, with a recapping of the preceding findings and a description of the rationale for moving on to the next set of topics. It is possible, nonetheless, to provide a general overview of the several topics at the outset.

Part one is devoted to the initial research concern which led to the survey: the allegation that medical science is undermining the humane values of medicine. To test this allegation, scientific orientations among the medical school faculty are examined, to distinguish the more scientific respondents from the less scientific. Once this has been accomplished, we turn to an examination of the influence of scientific orientations on several indicators of humane patient-physician relations. The findings of part one suggest that the relationship between science and morality is more complex than is commonly imagined.

Part two looks beyond specifically *medical* morality to consider the relationship between science and morality, more generally. The analysis focuses on the philosophical and moral bases of scientific orientations. Part two advances the thesis that the rise of medical science reflects, and is supported by, a broad shift in basic conceptions of the nature of man in society. It is contended that the traditional, individualistic morality of America's past is being replaced by a new social morality. Part two examines the nature of the new social morality, its relationship to science, and the joint effects of science and social morality on humane patient-physician relations.

Part three of the book considers the long-range implications of the new social morality, and other significant trends, for the future of humane medicine. During an era in which basic American and medical values are being reconsidered, we shall examine the sources of medical opinions regarding issues of medical morality. In this manner, we shall better appreciate the ways in which the future of medicine will be shaped.

Four appendixes at the back of the book provide additional technical information of possible interest to the reader. Appendix A is addressed to methodological issues. Appendix B is an informal biography of the project and offers as honest an account as I am able to provide of the manner in which the project was conducted and the final report prepared. Appendix C discusses the sample selection design and considers the representativeness of the faculty members participating in the study. Appendix D is a copy of the questionnaire used in the survey.

It should be clear that a work such as this reflects the invaluable support, assistance, and inspiration of many people and organizations. I am deeply indebted to all of these. First, I wish to thank the National Institute of Health for recognizing the need for research in this area and for providing the financial support which made it possible.

Second, an empirical study of this sort could not have been conducted but for the facilities and services of the Survey Research Center, Berkeley, and its staff. A new series of computer programs written by Charles Yarbrough during the course of this project made it possible to examine issues which might otherwise have been overlooked for lack of time and money. I am also grateful for the assistance provided by the Social Science Research Institute at the University of Hawaii. This final report should be regarded as a joint contribution of SRC and SSRI.

Special thanks are due to the participating medical colleges and to those faculty members who devoted their own time to the completion and return of the questionnaires. Without their cooperation, the study could never have been begun, let alone completed. The Association of American Medical Colleges assisted in administering pretests of the questionnaire, but did not participate in the final survey. Moreover, the association has asked us to specify that the final project does not have its official endorsement or approval.

There are many individuals who figured in the study's design, execution and analysis. On the medical side, my greatest thanks go to Professor Otto E. Guttentag, principal investigator and constant adviser. It was he who first appreciated the need for this research and who has spent several decades raising questions of medical ethics and medical philosophy.

On the sociological side, Professor Charles Y. Glock was the critical force in all stages of the study—from its earliest beginnings to the final reporting. Many of the sociological concepts examined in the analysis bear his personal stamp and were derived from a continuing dialogue with him. My debt to Professor Glock will perhaps only be understood and appreciated by others who have had the good fortune to work with him.

In view of their roles in connection with the development of this report, it is altogether fitting that Dr. Guttentag and Dr. Glock have appended a foreword and an afterword, respectively, to the book. Dr. Guttentag's foreword represents the initial medical concerns which generated the survey and discusses the survey findings in relation to those concerns.

Dr. Glock's afterword places the survey findings in a broad sociological perspective. His comments illustrate how a specific research concern can lead eventually to far more generalized concerns. I am deeply indebted to Dr. Glock and Dr. Guttentag for these additional contributions to the book. Their senses of perspective should add importantly to its potential utility.

Many other colleagues deserve special thanks. Dr. Alan Barbour and Dr. Paul Sanazaro offered valuable medical advice during the development of the study. During the analysis phase, Dr. Gertrude Selznick and Rodney Stark contributed greatly to my final conceptualization and understanding of the several dimensions and variables discussed. Others who contributed valuable comments, criticisms, and suggestions include Grant Barnes, Norman Bell, Fred Davis, Robert Feinbaum, Eliot Freidson, Gene Kassebaum, Patricia Kendall, William Nicholls, Neil Smelser, Stephen Steinberg, Martin Trow, and Charles Yarbrough.

Throughout the data collection and analysis phases, Sheila McLaughlin proved a valuable assistant. The job of typing working and final drafts was efficiently handled by Mary Chong, Anne Fogarty, Freda Hellinger, Beverly Johnson, Beth Shelbourne, and Carolyn Weick.

Finally, this book could never have appeared without the continuing encouragement and "comprehesive care" provided by my wife, Sheila. In addition to wifely forbearance, she went well beyond the call of duty by licking stamps, stuffing envelopes, discussing, and criticizing.

I have dedicated this report to my father, Herman O. Babbie, who died of a lingering fight with cancer during the course of the study, and to the chemotherapist who offered him both professional care and human compassion during those days of dying.

Science and Humane Patient Care

INTRODUCTION TO PART ONE

As this is being written, the popular press in America is filled with accounts of daring transplantations of hearts and other vital organs from one human body to another. Other reports tell of new machines capable of saving, sustaining, even reactivating life. Artificial limbs and organs now permit thousands of Americans to live and function despite serious failures or injuries of critical body parts. Truly, the past decade has provided a glimpse of the impressive potential of medical science to benefit mankind. Physicians and laymen alike are captivated by anticipations of the future.

These and other advances in medical science have brought about radical changes in the structure of the medical profession. None is more striking, however, than the decline of the general practitioner and his replacement by hosts of specialists. The growth of medical knowledge and techniques produced by scientific research during this century has made specialization evitable. No physician can hope to know everything about medicine today, and most have given up trying, preferring to concentrate their efforts in one segment of the profession. Thus, Bernhard Stern reports that between 1928 and 1942 the proportion of general practitioners in American medicine declined from 74 to 29 percent.[1]

In part, this shift represents a trend among physicians already in practice. Many who began as general practitioners have subsequently switched to specialties. In their study of the Class of 1915 at the University of Buffalo, Milton Terris and Mary Monk found that 3.8 percent were full-time specialists six years after graduation.[2] By 1950, however, this percentage had increased to more than half (53.8 percent).

For the most part, however, the trend toward specialization represents the changing orientations of succeeding generations of medical graduates. Thus, Aura E. Severinghaus notes that among medical school graduates during the first quarter of this century, 47 percent entered general practice.[3] But this percentage has decreased steadily, and during the period 1955 through 1964 only 19 percent chose this traditional medical career.

The change in orientations among medical school graduates is not simply a response to the changing times. Medical education itself seems to have the effect of decreasing students' interests in general practice and increasing those in specialization. When Patricia Kendall and Hanan Selvin examined the career aspirations of medical school students, they found 60 percent of the freshman class planning to enter general prac-

1. Bernhard J. Stern, "The Specialist and the General Practitioner," in *Patients, Physicians and Illness,* ed. E. Gartly Jaco (Glencoe, Ill.: Free Press, 1958), p. 354.
2. Milton Terris and Mary Monk, "Changes in Physicians' Careers: Relation of Time After Graduation to Specialization," in Jaco, *Patients, Physicians and Illness,* p. 363.
3. Aura E. Severinghaus, "Distribution of Graduates of Medical Schools in the United States and Canada According to Specialties, 1900 to 1964," *Journal of Medical Education* 40, no. 8 (August 1965), 733.

tice.[4] Among seniors, however, the percentage was only 16 percent.

There are many possible explanations for the trend toward specialization during medical training. Entering freshmen, for example, may be largely unfamiliar with the various specialities which may later attract them. Or, medical training may convince them of the difficulty of mastering all the knowledge required for competent general practice. Frustrated in the desire to know everything, a student may decide to focus on a particular speciality, hoping to learn at least one thing well.

While these explanations may be partially valid, the trend toward specialization among medical students represents more than mere numbers, and it represents more than the students' own decisions. First, the shift to specialization is most striking among the better students. Ironically, those students best qualified to attempt a general comprehension of medicine as a whole are the least likely to do so. The general practitioners of the future are being drawn disproportionately from the bottom of the class.

Kendall and Selvin provide documentation of this in their examination of internships taken by graduating medical students.[5] Among students in the top quartile of their class, 32 percent entered rotating internships (practically essential for general practice), while nearly three-fourths, 71 percent, of those in the bottom quartile did so.

Medical school faculty members, moreover, support the conclusion that general practice receives the poorest gradu-

4. Patricia L. Kendall and Hanan C. Selvin, "Tendencies Toward Specialization in Medical Training," in *The Student-Physician,* Robert K. Merton et al. (Cambridge, Mass.: Harvard University Press, 1957). See especially table 14 on p. 156. While these data refer to the sample of students examined at Cornell, the authors report that virtually the same results were obtained in their studies at the University of Pennsylvania and at Western Reserve.
5. *Ibid.,* table 19, p. 167.

ating students. The respondents in the present survey were asked to rate the overall quality of students at their colleges who entered careers in general practice. Only 5 percent rated such students as above average. When the same question was asked about students entering careers in specialized practice, 62 percent rated the latter as above average.[6]

Kendall and Selvin suggest, furthermore, that faculty members actively intervene in the career selection of medical students and encourage the brighter ones to forget about general practice and to consider specialization instead.

In other words, the high-ranking student at Cornell who maintains an interest in a rotating internship must to some extent go counter to the expectations and advice of the faculty and administration. . . . low-ranking students who indicated a preference for a specialized internship might be discouraged from actually applying for one, while, correlatively, high-ranking students who expressed interest in such specialized training might receive encouragement and support from the staff.[7]

In summary, general practice has been losing on all fronts. Within the medical profession as a whole, general practitioners are far outnumbered by specialists. All indications are for the trend to continue even farther toward specialization. Moreover, those students who do enter general practice are drawn disproportionately from the bottom of their classes. And there is evidence to suggest that medical school faculty members are intent on perpetuating these conditions.

It was mentioned at the outset that the trend toward specialization was, in part, a result of the impact of medical science. In a sense, it could be said that medical practice is becoming more scientific as a result. Specialized practitioners have a better grounding in the scientific bases of their speciali-

---

6. Ninety-four percent of the same respondents rated students entering academic medical careers as above average.
7. Kendall and Selvin, "Tendencies Toward Specialization," pp. 173–174.

ties than a general practitioner could ever hope to have regarding medicine as a whole. They are more qualified to keep up to date on sophisticated reports of complicated scientific experiments. And in a real sense, many specialists might be considered scientists in their own right. Some participate in research by providing data from their practices, while others conduct research projects of their own. It would appear, therefore, that the technical quality of medicine in the field, as in the laboratory, is being vastly improved.

Despite all this, many observers see a darker side to the ascendancy of science in medicine. They fear something is being lost in the rush to scientific achievement. This something, they suggest, is the physician's regard for his patient as a whole person, a total human being. Some say the increased emphases on science have depersonalized and segmented the patient and have made him something less than human—an object or a laboratory animal. Many argue, ironically, that the quality of medical practice has been reduced rather than increased.

Both specialization and medical science have been condemned roundly, often heatedly and emotionally. Increasingly, there are calls for a disavowal of science and a return to general practice. In those cases, the critics of science have generally been dismissed as sentimentalists or reactionaries. At the same time, however, some of the more progressive figures in medicine have begun to express concern about the movement to science. The points they raise are not so easily dismissed. The following two sections deal with some of the technical and moral grounds for concern now being expressed.

Technical Grounds for Concern

It has been characteristic of Western science to seek an understanding of a complex phenomenon through the isolation and observation of its constituent parts. Biologists, for example, reduce living organisms to organ systems, to organs, to tissues, and to cells. Organic cells are further reduced to subcellular structures, and so forth. The chemist describes the order of inorganic matter from natural compounds to elemental molecules and then to atoms and subatomic particles.

Western medical science has followed this same pattern with regard to man and the diseases which afflict him. Medical scientists have carved out limited areas for study, and specialists have sought to apply the findings relevant to those areas in medical practice. For example, some research scientists limit their investigations to cardiovascular diseases, and some specialists limit their attentions to treating such diseases. Seemingly such specialists ought to be able to provide more sophisticated care than physicians who attempt to deal with all disorders.

Nevertheless, the task of healing holds peculiar complications for specialization. The physician's task is to restore and maintain his patient's well-being. By this is meant the well-being of the patient as a whole. But as a physician in 1937 noted succinctly: "Patients seldom confine their illnesses to those of a single medical specialty." [8] At the very least then, a given specialist may not possess the skills necessary to ensure the total well-being of a given patient. Worse, he may not recognize those disorders which fall outside his particular speciality, concentrating only on that which is familiar to him.

In the past, of course, the general practitioner was responsible for the overall appraisal of the patient's condition. If he identified specific conditions which required intensive examination and treatment, he referred his patient to an appropriate specialist. Yet as we have seen, the general practitioner is vanishing from American medicine, and those who remain are poorly qualified, comparatively, for this role.

8. This quotation, from an anonymous physician, is presented in the large collection of medical opinions: *American Medicine: Expert Testimony Out of Court* (New York: American Foundation, 1937), p. 194.

The changing structure of medical care, then, is leading away from the comprehensive view of the patient as an integrated system. This is happening, moreover, at a time when physicians are becoming increasingly aware of the significant influence of nonsomatic factors in health. The development of psychosomatic medicine, for example, has shown the impact of psychological factors on bodily conditions. And more recently, physicians have become increasingly concerned with the influence of the social milieu—such as family, job, community, religion—on the patient's health. On the one hand, then, there is growing awareness of the necessity to view the patient as an integrated physical and psychological system within a social milieu, while on the other hand, the structure of medical care has been evolving in exactly the opposite direction.

The traditional general practitioner often possessed the comprehensive knowledge about his patients which is now felt to be essential for effective care. His patients were his friends rather than simply his clients. He knew the patient's life history, his family, his job, and his role in the community. Moreover, it would appear that many general practitioners employed such information in the diagnosis and treatment of their patients. They recognized those cases where compassion and understanding would be more therapeutic than drugs or surgery. They realized, perhaps, that the treatment prescribed for the farmer would not be appropriate for the spinster schoolteacher. They sensed these things intuitively, for they lived with their patients as friends and neighbors. The contemporary, specialized practitioner, by contrast, is not likely to possess such comprehensive information about his patients.

A greater concern, however, is that many of the younger, scientifically oriented specialists do not even recognize this loss. Since the comprehensive view of patients is so closely associated with the traditional general practitioner of rural

America, many young physicians may regard it as merely a relic of the past. Caught up in the concerns of their own speciality, they may become convinced that their advanced, specialized treatments are sufficient.

Many critics suggest that scientific emphases create a frame of mind which effectively rules out the comprehensive view of patients. Not only does scientific research focus attention on ever more specified segments of the patient, it also shifts that attention from the patient to the disease itself. The great strides in recording and organizing disease syndromes have generated an orientation to disease as an entity in itself. As various disease syndromes have become better documented and their etiologies more rationally understood, these diseases have been assigned ontological beings of their own. People sometimes speak of disease "striking" a person, as though he had been attacked by a living creature, or speak of a man "having cancer" (as though the disease had entered his body) rather than say that some of his tissues had become cancerous.

From such a perspective, the disease, rather than the patient, becomes the focus of the physician's efforts. In many instances, of course, this approach is the most appropriate. In others, though, it is not, and critics of science in medicine fear that modern physicians will not be able to distinguish the two types of cases.

In summary, we have seen that there are legitimate reasons for concern, on technical grounds, over the rapid growth of specialization in medical practice. The organic unity of the human body, the influence of the patient's psyche, and his social environment present peculiar difficulties for the scientific differentiation of function which has benefited other sectors of life. Ultimately, the physician is responsible for restoring and maintaining the health of the patient as a whole person. Specialization restricts the collection of information relevant to that task, and some would contend that a scientific orientation even blinds the physician to the desirability of such information.

Moral Grounds for Concern

While the technical grounds for concern have been presented and debated rationally and unemotionally in medical literature, the same cannot be said of the moral grounds for concern. Typical of the tone of these comments was the condemnation of creeping specialization by a 1937 physician who warned that "in place of the good old family physician, guide and counselor we shall have an uninterested, impersonal and to that extent cold-blooded indifferent and mechanical stranger." [9] The previous section dealt with the concern that scientific, specialized medicine may be ineffective; the present section deals with the charge that it is immoral and inhumane.

For the most part, the moral grounds for concern are expressed with regard to the relationship which ought to exist between the physician and his patient. The ideal relationship which many cite is the one which is believed to have existed in the days of the general practitioner in family practice.

Now in the old days the doctor sat beside your bed and held your hand and that doctor-patient relationship meant something. Every family had its own doctor and next to the minister, he was the closest friend the family had. They believed in him absolutely and when you got sick and he came and held your hand as your friend, it meant something to you. Now that has gone. It has all gone. . . . [10]

Comments like this one speak of a vague something which is missing from contemporary, scientific, medical care. In

9. *Ibid.*, p. 192.
10. Robert N. Wilson quotes this elderly lady regarding her recollections as a hospital administrator in an earlier era. "The Physician's Hospital Role," in *Medical Care: Readings in the Sociology of Medical Institutions,* eds. W. Richard Scott and Edmund H. Volkart (New York: John Wiley & Sons, 1966), pp. 414–415.

part, that something is the physician as a friend. Many concerned observers speak of his "bedside manner." Often, as in the example above, reference is made to the physician holding the patient's hand. Indeed, the nostalgic and prosaic character of such comments has led many scientifically oriented physicians to dismiss them as softheaded nonsense. "A kindly smile, a gentle pat and a benevolent disposition hardly take the place of careful examination, thorough study and a scientific skepticism. . . ." [11]

Unhappily, this issue has for too long been debated as an either/or proposition: either scientific care or humane and compassionate care. Immature spokesmen for both sides have suggested that only one is really necessary. And in the eyes of both groups, there has been a general movement in the direction of science.

In the midst of this emotional debate, more rational voices have suggested that both science and compassion are desirable for effective medical care. In a scientific age, many progressive medical figures are calling for a reappraisal of the nonscientific aspects of the physician's personal relations with his patients. They suggest that medicine has an important moral component even, perhaps especially, in an age of enormous scientific achievement.

Why are interpersonal relations considered so important in medicine? The patient-physician relationship, like other social relationships, reflects the general values of human morality in a given society. Those values, in turn, are founded on basic ontological beliefs about man's nature and that of society. The character of the relations between physicians and their patients, then, ultimately supports or threatens the basic beliefs held in the general society.

An important keystone of American society since its founding has been a belief in the inherent worth of the individual.

11. American Foundation, *American Medicine,* p. 188.

The major value-systems of our society are grounded in this belief. American religion has traditionally stressed the individual's responsibility to God rather than to a corporate church. American political values emphasize the inviolability of the individual's "life, liberty and pursuit of happiness." And the traditionally capitalistic economic values place a high priority on individual opportunities and individual responsibilities in the marketplace.

Specified social relations in America have reflected, more often than not, this basic belief in the value of the individual human being and the value systems which support that belief. Because of its direct influence over human life and health, the medical profession has been particularly sensitive to this issue. The inherent value of human life has seriously limited experimentations which might endanger one life while potentially saving thousands. Confronted with a suffering patient who faces certain death, the physician is prevented from speeding up the process, even when the patient desires it. And, in theory at least, incompetent medical treatment is openly censured regardless of who the unfortunate victim may have been.

The sanctity of the individual human being is reflected in less dramatic medical situations as well. Indeed, in all his interpersonal relations with his patients, the physician is expected to treat them with all the respect and consideration due a human being in American society. Abstract formulations of what this means in practice are hard to come by, but three norms stand out as particularly important. (1) Medical relations should be *social* relations in that the physician identifies his patient as a human being rather than as an animal or an object. (2) The physician accepts a sacred trust for the patient's well-being; his responsibility is not to be taken lightly or acted upon halfheartedly. (3) Recognizing that he is interacting with human beings in trying and dangerous circumstances, the physician should indicate to them his feelings of compassion and human concern for the successful execution of his responsibilities.

The traditional general practitioner in rural America is frequently cited as a prototype of these norms in practice. First, he regarded his patients as human beings, for as we noted above, they were often his friends and neighbors. Second, his ultimate responsibility for his patients was evident in the fact that he was probably the only physician available, and a wealth of anecdotal material suggests that he took his responsibility seriously. Finally, he felt compassion and concern for his success, for to lose a patient was, perhaps, to lose a friend.

These are the ways, we are told, that the general practitioner demonstrated his commitment to the basic American belief in the inherent worth of the individual human being. Not even the most starry-eyed and nostalgic among us would suggest that all general practitioners lived up to this ideal portrayal all the time. Yet, there are legitimate grounds for fearing that the structure of specialized practice and the scientific perspective may have undermined these three basic norms of the patient-physician relationship.

Ideally, science is amoral.[12] It is concerned with questions of true and false, not good and evil. The rational-empirical principles of the scientific method can say nothing about the proper relations which ought to exist among man. Nevertheless, science is not wholly unrelated to such concerns.

As noted earlier in this section, conceptions of human morality are based on ontological beliefs about the nature of man and of society. Those basic beliefs are held as facts through faith and tradition. Yet facts are the stock-in-trade of science, and its methods for determining facts have historically undermined or displaced all other methods. At its very base, then, science presents a threat to systems of morality.

12. This does not mean, however, that scientists are or need to be amoral.

The scientific perspective, and the specialized practice related to it, pose a more specific threat to the morality of traditional medical care, based on the sanctity of the individual. First, they threaten the norm which holds that the physician must regard his patient as a human being. In scientific terms, this norm asserts that the total human being is the "unit of analysis." Yet scientists would argue that there are always several possible units of analysis. And as noted above, the total human being is seldom the unit of analysis for scientific medical research and specialized medical practice. More often, the unit of analysis is an organ, a tissue, a disease syndrome. Or it might be a class of human beings, perhaps a sociomedical type such as smokers or nonsmokers.

There is an inherent danger, then, that the scientifically oriented specialist, when confronted with a patient, may view and treat him as an object or a social type rather than as a total human being. This danger seems even greater in the case of human experimentation in medical research. The Nazi experience provides a fortunately rare, though horribly vivid, example of this orientation in excess. By their own admissions, the concentration camp experimenters held their subjects to be no more sacred than guinea pigs. Science per se does not recognize the special sanctity of the human individual. Individual human beings represent only one possible unit of analysis and often an inappropriate one.

Second, there are grounds for believing that science and specialization may undermine the physician's traditional acceptance of responsibility for his patient's well-being. In the simplest case, the specialized practitioner who defines his sector of professional attention as a specific organ or disease syndrome might logically be expected to define his responsibility in similar terms. He might very well feel his responsibility extended only to the successful removal of a malignant tumor from the patient's lung. The patient's total recovery and readjustment to his life situation might be left to someone else, or to no one.

More dramatically, an example of a possible clinical research project illustrates the threat of science to both the first and second norms of traditional medical morality. Let us assume for the moment that a medical researcher has developed what he believes to be an effective therapeutic technique. He wishes to test its efficacy among hospital patients suffering from the disease it is designed to cure. To begin, he will wish to divide the patients into two groups by a random assignment. Quite conceivably, the attending physicians of some patients would refuse to accept this procedure, but we shall assume the researcher has been successful in persuading them to cooperate. One group of patients is to receive the new therapy while the other group receives a currently accepted therapy. The effectiveness of the new therapy will be determined by the relative recovery of the two groups.

The experiment is begun. After a few weeks or months, the experimenter discovers that patients in one group are recovering much faster than the others. Regardless of which therapy is proving more effective, old or new, a moral dilemma is created. The researcher's responsibility as a scientist calls for the completion of the experiment. Unless it runs out the length of time specified in the study design, he must hold his conclusions somewhat in abeyance. Given the differential recovery rates of the two groups, however, it is likely that the attending physicians of patients in the slower recovery group will call for the termination of the experiment. They will define their responsibilities in terms of the safe recovery of their particular patients. (It seems likely that pressure for the termination of the experiment will be all the greater in those cases where the new therapy is proving less effective.)

If one of the patients were to die during the course of the

experiment, this event would constitute important data for what the experimenter might consider a totally successful experiment. To the patient's attending physician, however, this event would constitute total failure. Henry Beecher has nicely summarized this difference in professional orientations: "The physician *accepts* patients and is mainly concerned with their welfare; the investigator *selects* subjects (problems as well as individuals) and while responsive to the patient's interest, is bent on solving the scientific problem." [13]

Ultimately, both of these orientations are necessary for an effective medical profession as a whole. Yet the overall shift of orientations in the direction of science would appear to undermine the traditional responsibility for the individual patient. In the extreme, if all physicians were scientifically oriented, would anyone care what happened to the patients being studied and supposedly cared for?

Finally, the scientific perspective would seem to undermine the traditional norm of compassion and human concern in medical care. Objectivity is one of the keystones of science. The scientist is expected to limit his attention to the empirical examination of those variables relevant to his investigations; his human emotions are, at best, irrelevant and, at worst, dysfunctional and damaging.

In this regard, the scientist is poles apart from the traditional general practitioner whose patients were his friends whose suffering he often felt personally. The specialist is also a variation from the traditional pattern. Like the scientist, he also limits his attention and his responsibility to a part of the patient rather than extends them to the whole person. In large part, his duties may involve consultation and assistance with regard to patients he has never met before. In these circum-

13. Henry Beecher, *Experimentation in Man* (Springfield, Ill.: Charles C Thomas, 1958), p. 23.

stances, there seems a good possibility that compassion and concern will play a smaller part in his activities.

These, then, are the grounds for moral concern over the trend toward science in American medicine. Often these concerns are expressed emotionally and involve a total condemnation of medical science. As such they are generally dismissed by scientifically oriented physicians without much serious attention. Hopefully, the above discussion will have pointed out the legitimate grounds for concern. Potentially, at least, science threatens to undermine the basic morality of American medical care. In so doing, it poses a threat to the traditional American belief in the inherent worth of the individual human being.

Countertrends in Medical Education

The trend toward science in medicine is most often related to changes in the nation's medical colleges. Early in this century, Abraham Flexner conducted a study of medical education for the Carnegie Foundation. His report was one of the most damning the medical profession has ever suffered. Among other shortcomings, he found that the quality of scientific instruction was deplorably low. Many medical colleges had no laboratory equipment, others had only outdated and inoperable junk. The Flexner report caused a good deal of discussion among medical educators and became the conceptual basis for restructuring the entire field of scientific medical education. Indeed, the field was completely revolutionized by the report.

In the half-century which has followed that report, more money and talent have been poured into this aspect of medical training than any other. Of the ninety million dollars spent in the construction of medical school facilities in 1963–64, over fifty-eight million was for research facilities. Of the eleven million dollars spent on equipment, over eight million went for the purchase of research equipment.[14] Today, much if not most of the impressive advances in medical science take place in modern, well-financed university research laboratories.

Undergraduate medical education has also changed in accord with the Flexner report. More emphasis has been placed on training in the basic sciences. Typically, undergraduates have spent their first two years learning the scientific bases of medicine and have dealt with patients only in their third and fourth years. In an age of rapid medical scientific advances, the aim of this educational pattern has been to produce a group of young physicians who are capable of effectively utilizing in practice what medical science has created in the laboratory.

It is precisely this educational pattern, however, which has generated many of the criticisms discussed earlier. The emphasis on basic science, especially in the formative years, leads students to reconceive their chosen profession as a purely scientific endeavor, we are told. When students finally deal with patients during their third and fourth years, those patients are regarded in terms of the scientific issues which comprised the first two years of the medical curriculum. And, as Henry Packer notes, the nature of patient contacts in medical school reinforces this orientation.

The episodic character of most contacts made by students with patients frequently results in a preoccupation with the organic pathology without consideration or understanding of the total problem of the patient. The latter is difficult to visualize without an opportunity of seeing the patient in his usual environment, outside the hospital, and observing the influence of family life and socio-economic factors upon the patient's health or illness.[15]

14. These figures are taken from the report prepared by the staff of the Council on Medical Education (AAMC), *Medical Education in the United States,* reprinted from *Journal of the American Medical Association* 190, no. 7 (November 16, 1964), p. 599.
15. Henry Packer, "Family Care Programs in Medical Education," *Southern Medical Journal* 47, no. 7 (July 1954), p. 689.

In response to such appraisals of medical education, based on both the technical and moral concerns discussed above, a number of innovations have appeared to counterbalance the possible dangers of the scientific emphases in contemporary medicine. Programs of "comprehensive care" are the best known and most extensively instituted innovation.[16] Although the specific structures of such programs vary from school to school, the basic format includes earlier and more intensive student contacts with patients. For example, students may be assigned their own patients in the university outpatient department. Working under the supervision of a faculty member, they meet with their patients at the university, participate in diagnosis and in the development of therapeutic measures, and follow the progress of the patients afterwards. Often, the students participating in such programs are encouraged to make house calls on their patients. This provides them an opportunity to meet the patient's family and to learn something of the total environment to which the patient is readjusting.

Programs of comprehensive care, then, are designed to counter both the technical and moral concerns generated by the rise of scientific medicine. Through intensive and extended treatment of a particular patient, the student is afforded an opportunity to learn the necessity of considering all aspects of the patient and his environment in the task of healing. At the same time, it is hoped that students will regard their patients as total human beings rather than as clinical examples of disease syndromes. In this manner, the traditional norms of responsibility and compassion may be maintained.

Other medical school programs have been aimed directly

16. An excellent description of the variety of comprehensive care programs may be found in Parnie S. Snoke and E. Richard Weinerman, "Comprehensive Care Programs in University Medical Centers," *Journal of Medical Education*, July 1965, pp. 625–657.

at the previously discussed trend toward specialization and the decline of general practice. One example was the program of "Family Care" (now defunct) at the University of Tennessee College of Medicine. This program was organized to provide family-care experience for those students planning careers in general practice and to broaden the viewpoints of those planning to specialize; and for those undecided about their ultimate career plans, the program "might conceivably bring to light a natural inclination toward family practice, for which recruits are badly needed." [17] To these ends, medical students were assigned as assistants to general practitioners in the community.

Other responses to the perceived problem have taken a more didactic form. With regard to the technical concern, several medical schools have instituted courses and programs of study in the behavioral sciences. Through formal courses in fields such as psychology and sociology, it is hoped that students can be shown that practical medical care must be grounded in a full understanding of the patient's total life situation. Furthermore, such courses provide students with information and the tools for getting information relevant to the nonsomatic aspects of health and illness. This response represents an attempt to formalize much of what was formerly regarded as the "art" of medicine.[18]

A didactic response has also been suggested with regard to the moral concerns generated by scientific medicine. In 1960, Otto E. Guttentag suggested the establishment of a course entitled "The Medical Attitude." "Instruction dealing with such questions as what does it mean to be a physician, what is the philosophical relationship between medicine and the other professions, what is the structure of the patient-physician relation-

17. Packer, "Family Care Programs," p. 690.
18. See, for example, Samuel W. Bloom, *The Doctor and His Patient* (New York: Russell Sage Foundation, 1963).

ship, is lacking from nearly all current medical curricula." [19]
The course which Guttentag proposed dealt directly with such
moral questions as were discussed above: the physician's regard for his patient as a fellow human being, responsibility for
the patient, and the need for compassion and human concern.

These, then, are some of the many educational responses
to the rise of scientific medicine in America. There is probably
no medical faculty in the country that does not at least discuss
the technical and moral concerns involved. Many have taken
steps to act on those concerns.

The Present Study

This book, also, represents a concern for the implications
of scientific medicine, but at the same time it represents a concern for the countertrends in medicine as well. Specifically,
part one examines the validity of the *moral* concerns expressed
above: does science actually undermine the traditional norms
of humane medical care?

This report does not deal with the *technical* concerns discussed in the preceding pages, and a word of explanation is in
order. The need for comprehensive knowledge as the basis for
effective medical care is beyond question. Further, I believe
that the segmentation inherent in the scientific perspective en-
dangers medical care in that regard, and the trend toward science should be counterbalanced by new emphases on comprehensive and integrated views of the patient and applications of
medical knowledge. How this should be accomplished, whether
existing programs are sufficient, is not for the sociologist to say.
Only physicians are technically qualified to render these judg-

19. Otto E. Guttentag, "A Course Entitled 'The Medical Attitude,'" *Journal
of Medical Education* 35, no. 10 (October 1960), p. 903. For a more
detailed discussion of the ethical aspects of human experimentation, see
Otto E. Guttentag, "Ethical Problems in Human Experimentation,"
Ethical Issues in Medicine, E. Fuller Torrey, ed., Boston: Little, Brown
and Company, 1968, pp. 196–226.

ments. The technical concerns have been examined in this introduction for the sole purpose of distinguishing them from the moral concerns which constitute the focus of the book. In the medical and sociomedical literature, these two concerns are often interwoven, and it will be necessary to separate them if we are to understand either.

Turning to the specifically *moral* concerns, it is impossible to find more than anecdotal evidence to support the allegation that science is undermining the traditional morality of humane medical care. While the theoretical grounds for believing this to be true may be substantial, there is no empirical evidence to support them. Part one of this book is devoted specifically to an empirical test of the allegations, to replace speculation with a few facts.

Chapter one begins by examining scientific orientations among the sample of teaching physicians. A series of questions asked of respondents juxtaposed interests in patient care and interests in scientific medical research. Faculty responses to these questions provide a gauge of the extent to which new, scientific concerns have displaced the traditional concerns for patient care. Several of the questions are then combined in the construction of a composite measure of scientific orientations. This measure permits us to distinguish, comparatively, the scientific from the nonscientific faculty members. The conclusion of chapter one provides a tentative appraisal of the trend toward scientific orientations among faculty members.

The scientists having been distinguished from the nonscientists, chapter two tests the allegation that scientific faculty members will be less committed to the traditional norms of humane medical care. Specifically, three propositions are tested: (*a*) that scientific faculty members are less compassionate in patient-care situations, (*b*) that scientific members are more irresponsible in the care of patients assigned to them, and (*c*) that scientific faculty members are more likely to disregard the human quality of patients who serve as experimental subjects in medical research.

While these analyses surely do not provide a final and conclusive test of the allegations directed against scientific medicine, they offer a beginning in that direction. More important, they will demonstrate the need for a somewhat more sophisticated understanding of contemporary American medicine. The remainder of the book will then attempt to sketch out the additional issues that must be considered.

CHAPTER ONE

Measuring Scientific Orientations

Who Are the Teaching Physicians?

The analyses and discussions which constitute this book are based on the questionnaire responses of 454 full-time faculty members in Medicine and Pediatrics at twelve of the nation's medical colleges. Appendix C describes the manner in which these faculty members were selected and offers a verification of their representatives. Before turning to their scientific orientations, however, it will be useful to present a descriptive overview of the men and women we shall be discussing throughout the book.

The sample of teaching physicians contains all academic ranks. Fifteen percent are instructors, 36 percent are assistant professors, 25 percent are associate professors, and the remaining 24 percent are full professors.

Medicine in the United States is predominantly a male profession, and this fact is reflected in the sex composition of the sample. Ninety-two percent of the respondents are men. Furthermore, it is interesting to note that only one respondent in ten is not married. By and large they are young: 27 percent are thirty-five or under, 47 percent are between thirty-six and forty-five, and another 21 percent are forty-six to fifty-five. Only 5 percent are over fifty-five years of age.

Although they come from all over the country, most were brought up in the East (41 percent) and the Midwest (24 percent). Sixteen percent report growing up in the South, and 9 percent are from the West. Ten percent of the teaching physicians were raised outside the United States—predominantly in Europe. More interesting than their regional origins, however, are their urban roots. The majority (56 percent) were raised in cities of 100,000 or more population; indeed, one respondent in five reports growing up in a city of one million or more. By contrast, only 6 percent were raised in small farming communities, and another 14 percent grew up in towns of less than 10,000.

As a summary characterization, then, the respondents are modally young, married men with urban roots in either the East or the Midwest. Let us turn now to an examination of their orientations to science.

AN OVERVIEW OF FACULTY ORIENTATIONS

A central element in the debate over the impact of science in medicine is the charge that faculty members have become so interested in scientific problems that they have lost all interest in the traditional concerns of patient care. This exclusive concern for science is then passed on to medical students, we are told.

This first section will provide a descriptive overview of the professional orientations of the teaching physicians who participated in the study. A series of questions asked respondents to indicate their primary medical interests. The replies to each of those questions provide an insight into faculty members' relative interests in the traditional issues of patient care versus scientific interests. Thus, we can discover the extent to which science has displaced patient care as the focus of faculty attention.

Having examined faculty interests in terms of their answers to individual questions, we shall then combine their responses to create a composite index of scientific orientations. This composite index will be used in turn to test the allegations regarding the effects of science on the traditional norms of humane patient-physician relations.

Perceived Teaching Contributions

As faculty members in the clinical departments of Medicine and Pediatrics, the respondents to this study are charged with responsibility for training medical students both in patient care and in medical research relevant to such care. As instructors, they are called upon to appear before students in two roles: physician and scientist. It seems likely, however, that each faculty member feels more inclined toward one role than toward the other. To determine these different inclinations, respondents were asked: "As a medical school faculty member, in what capacity do you feel you can make your greatest *teaching* contribution: as a practicing physician or as a medical researcher?"

In response to this question, roughly two-thirds said their greatest teaching contribution was in the role of practicing physician. This finding would seem to contradict the allegation that medical faculty members have given up their concern with patient care in favor of science. There are two possible explanations, however, for the reluctance of faculty members to identify themselves as researchers.

First, we must recall that the teaching physcians in this study are all members in the clinical departments of Medicine and Pediatrics. Surely, a much different pattern of responses would have been found in a sample of endocrinologists or pathologists. Second, evidence to be introduced later in this chapter suggests that the faculty members attach a rather restricted meaning to the term "medical researcher." Many of the respondents are engaged in what they themselves would argue is scientific, medical research, yet they are reluctant to identify themselves as researchers.

Faculty Duty Preferences

The university duties performed by faculty members vary broadly, including care of patients, research, and teaching. Often, they find themselves performing duties they do not particularly enjoy. The survey questionnaire asked them to indicate the kinds of duties they would prefer if the choice were completely theirs. "If you could plan the pattern of your duties as a medical school instructor, which one of the following do you feel would be the most enjoyable for you?"

The five answers provided for respondents were designed to tap orientations to research in contrast to the traditional concerns for patient care. One response was: "Doing basic research in clinical medicine." This, of course, would indicate a renunciation of patient-care duties in favor of the laboratory. It is this response which many critics of medical education would expect most faculty members to select.

Two of the answers provided in the questionnaire combined patient care and research: "Caring for patients and researching those problems which were involved in their care," and "Doing research in total patient symptomatology and developing better diagnostic techniques and treatments." Selecting one of these responses would indicate an interest in research but not the exclusive interest inherent in the first response.

The two remaining choices involved only patient care and the training of others in patient care: "Caring for patients and using particular patients to illustrate pathological processes to students," and "Supervising students and house staff in the care of patients." One imagines the critics of medical education would expect few faculty members to choose one of these latter responses.

TABLE 1
FACULTY DUTY PREFERENCES

Question: If you could plan the pattern of your duties as a medical school instructor, which *one* of the following do you feel would be the most enjoyable for you?	Percentage
Doing basic research in clinical medicine........................	24
Doing research in total patient symptomatology and developing better diagnostic techniques and treatments.......................	8
Caring for patients and researching those problems which were involved in their care...	32
Caring for patients and using particular patients to illustrate pathological processes to students...............................	14
Supervising students and house staff in the care of patients...........	22
	100% = (436)*

* Eighteen faculty members failed to answer this question. The percentages are computed on the basis of the 436 who did answer it.

Table 1 presents the responses faculty members gave to this question. Only 24 percent chose duties devoted exclusively to research and devoid of patient care. Forty percent chose duties which combined both research and care, while the remaining 36 percent avoided research altogether in their selection.

At the very least, these responses do not represent a total commitment to scientific interests among medical school faculty members. Three-fourths of the respondents indicate a continuing concern for patient care. At the same time, it is possible to read these results in the other direction: one-fourth of these *clinical department* faculty members would prefer to avoid patient care altogether.

Ultimate Medical Interests

These first two questions dealt with the roles faculty members might play in medical education. Three other questions considered their personal interests regarding their own continuing education. The first asked: "As you continue to advance your own medical knowledge, would you say your ultimate medical interests lie primarily in the direction of total patient management, or the understanding of basic mechanisms?"

To many observers, this choice is the basic one. The traditional concern of physicians has been with total patient management, the overall healing of the total human being. As we have noted earlier, science is based on the understanding of the basic mechanisms of the body and the diseases which afflict it. The common allegation is that medical faculty members have become wholly committed to the latter perspecive.

The responses provided by the sample of teaching physicians supports this allegation, at least in part. Nearly two-thirds (63 percent) say they are more concerned with understanding basic mechanisms than with learning more about total patient management.

Reading Preferences

The second question dealing with faculty members' continuing education asked about their preferences for articles in medical journals. Since the quantity of professional literature available to them is both vast and diverse, they must read selectively. The type of articles they select provides a further indication of relative orientations to science or to patient care.

Faculty were asked: "In the field of therapeutic research, are you generally more interested in articles reporting evaluations of the effectiveness of various treatments or articles exploring the basic rationale underlying the treatments?" The implications of responses to this question are clear. All clinical faculty members are interested in the effectiveness of new methods of healing. Yet it is to be expected that the more scientifically oriented faculty would express a greater interest in understanding the rationale behind such treatments.

Overall, only 18 percent of the faculty members said they were primarily interested in articles dealing with the effectiveness of treatments. The remainder prefer to know *why* a treatment is effective rather than *how* effective it is. This latest finding, then, strongly supports the allegation of a predominant faculty commitment to scientific orientations.

Lecture Preferences

The third question dealing with faculty interests regarding their own continuing education examined preferences for different lecture topics which might be presented in the university hospital. The question read: "Suppose the following lectures were offered in your hospital: . . . Which 2 would interest you most?" The lectures were:

"Group Practice—Pros and Cons"
"Office Treatment of Thyroid Disorders"
"Lipid Metabolism"
"How to Avoid Malpractice Suits"
"Stimulants and Sedatives"
"The Role of Serotonin in Disorders of the Gut"

Half of the teaching physicians in the sample (49 percent) selected "Lipid Metabolism" and "The Role of Serotonin in Disorders of the Gut" as their two choices, indicating a strongly scientific orientation. The remainder gave either mixed answers or answers oriented exclusively to the practice of medicine rather than to medical science.

Preference for Faculty Experience

Finally, respondents were asked to comment on the professional experience they considered most appropriate training for full-time faculty members in the clinical departments of Medicine and Pediatrics. In reaction to the perceived overemphasis on science in medical education, it has often been suggested that more experienced practitioners should be used as instructors. The teaching physicians in the present survey do not agree, however.

When asked "Which of the following would you consider the best practical training for a *full-time* faculty member in your department?" 58 percent answered "experience as a medical scientist." About half as many chose "experience as a specialized practitioner." One respondent in ten said "experience as a basic science investigator" as the best practical training." The remaining 3 percent preferred "experience as a general practitioner."

Overall, then, the sample of teaching physicians strongly support the role of scientists in medical education—even in the clinical departments of Medicine and Pediatrics. This finding agrees with the expectations expressed by many critics of contemporary medical education in America.

AN INDEX OF SCIENTIFIC ORIENTATIONS

The preceding descriptive examination of responses to the survey questionnaire provides an overview of faculty orientations to science as opposed to the traditional concerns for patient care. On some items, the faculty respondents, as a group, appear strongly oriented to science, while on others their predominant interest lies with patient care. Since there is no absolute standard against which to judge these findings, each reader must decide for himself whether the overall profile of orientations represents too great a commitment to science, too little, or just the right balance of scientific and patient-care concerns.

More important for our purposes, the examination has shown that faculty members differ in their orientations to science. Their answers to each of the questions provide a basis for distinguishing the more scientifically oriented faculty from those less scientifically oriented. The central aim of the following chapter will be to determine the effects of scientific orientations on the traditional norms of humane patient care. To do this, we must first distinguish scientists from nonscientists among the sample of faculty members. Then we shall be in a position to compare the two groups in terms of their commitments to the traditional norms of humane care.

The manner in which the two groups are distinguished is therefore critical. Probably none of the questions discussed above provides a perfect reflection of scientific orientations. No matter which item might be selected, some faculty members would be misidentified. At the same time, each item provides a partial indication of faculty orientations. The responses given to one item are related, in varying degrees, to the responses given to others. In view of this, we shall create a composite index of scientific orientations which combines faculty responses to several questions.

Three of the items discussed above have been selected for this purpose—perceived teaching contributions, ultimate medical interests, and reading preferences. Each of these questions has clear face-validity as a measure of scientific orientations. At the same time, however, each taps a slightly different aspect of scientific orientations. The first—perceived teaching contributions—measures faculty self-identifications: as practicing physicians or as medical researchers. The second—ultimate medical interests—taps the basic intellectual orientations to either total patient management or the understanding of basic mechanisms. The third—reading preferences—comes closer to measuring "orientations in action" by asking faculty members how they distribute their reading time among different types of articles.

That the three items tap slightly different aspects of scientific orientations is further substantiated when we recall the different overall responses each question evoked. In terms of the first, only about one-third of the teaching physicians would be classified as science-oriented. The second item would so classify two-thirds, while four out of five would qualify as science-oriented in terms of the third item.

Despite these differences, however, the three items all tap the same general dimension—scientific orientations. This is evident in the trivariate relationship presented in table 2, which shows the joint effects of faculty reading preferences and perceived teaching contributions in predicting their ultimate medical interests.

TABLE 2

READING PREFERENCE AND PERCEIVED TEACHING CONTRIBUTION AS PREDICTORS OF ULTIMATE MEDICAL INTERESTS

	Percentage most interested in basic mechanisms	
	Perceived teaching contribution	
Reading preference	Physician	Researcher
Effectiveness	27 (66)	58 (12)
Rationale	58 (219)	89 (130)

Note: Number in parentheses represents number of cases on which percentage is based.

Table 2 presents the simultaneous interaction of responses to the three questions. Faculty members have been arranged in four groups according to their reading preference and their perceptions regarding the roles in which they can make their greatest teaching contributions. For each of the four groups, the percentage who express an ultimate interest in basic mechanisms is shown.

Reading across the table, it is apparent that whatever their reading preferences, faculty members who selected the role of researcher are more interested in basic mechanisms than are those who selected the role of practicing physician. And, reading down the columns, reading preferences are still related to ultimate medical interests regardless of the role faculty members selected.

Two additional observations should be made regarding table 2. First, there is the cumulative effect of reading preferences and role selection on ultimate medical interests. Of those 66 faculty members not oriented to science in terms of either their reading preferences or their role selections, only one-fourth are interested in basic mechanisms. On the other hand, among those oriented toward science in both respects, 89 percent have this ultimate interest; only 11 percent have a greater interest in learning about total patient management.

Second, the *relative* effects of reading preferences and role selections on ultimate medical interests should also be noted: they are identical. The effect of reading preferences on medical interests is the same (31 percentage points) no matter which role was selected. And role selection has this same effect on medical interests whatever the respondent's preference for medical articles. The symmetry of effects is clearest with respect to the two mixed cases in the table. Among faculty members who are oriented to science on one item but not on the other, 58 percent are interested in basic mechanisms, regardless of which response pattern they chose.

Other evidence might be introduced to substantiate the belief that the three items being examined provide an excellent cumulative measure of scientific orientations. We noted above that each item produced a different pattern of responses. It may also be added that the combined response patterns on all three produce a Guttman-type scale. The *number* of science-oriented responses given by a faculty member provides a very strong indication of *which* science-oriented responses were given.[1]

These, then, are the grounds for selecting three particular items for the construction of a composite index of scientific orientations. The other items examined at the outset are, assuredly, indicators of scientific orientations, but they are not suited for inclusion in a composite index. In some instances, the effects of one item were severely reduced by the introduction of another. Some combinations of items produced so skewed a distribution of cases that the resultant index scores would have denied further analysis. Other combinations seemed to produce a distorted conceptualization of scientific orientations—contrasted with the prima facie balance provided by the three items which were selected.

In short, the three items selected are nicely matched to one another for the construction of a composite index of scientific orientations. Therefore faculty members were given one point for each answer which indicated an orientation toward science and zero for each answer which did not. The index created in this fashion, then, ranged from a low score of *0*, which represented a scientific orientation on none of the items, to a high score of *3*, representing a scientific orientation on all three.[2]

Validation of the Index

Although the composite index has been seen to be internally consistent, one more step is necessary before it can be accepted as an accurate measure of scientific orientations. If the index is a good one, we should expect to find it a powerful mechanism for predicting faculty responses to other items that also reflect scientific orientations.

1. See the methodological notes in Appendix A for an examination of the scalability of the items.
2. The methodological notes in Appendix A describe the index construction in greater detail.

To begin, table 3 shows that scores on the index of scientific orientations are closely related to the faculty duties which the respondents expressed an interest in. We recall that faculty were asked to select from a list of five duties—varying from an exclusive involvement in research to an exclusive involvement in patient care.

TABLE 3

SCIENTIFIC ORIENTATION INDEX AS A PREDICTOR OF DUTY PREFERENCES

	Index of Scientific Orientations			
	Low 0	1	2	High 3
Types of duties preferred				
Research only	0%	8%	32%	66%
Care and research	35	40	34	21
Patient care only	65	52	34	13
	(46)	(115)	(145)	(113)

Note: Number in parentheses represents number of cases on which percentage is based.

Among faculty scored lowest (*0*) on scientific orientations none expressed a preference for the duty involving research solely. This percentage increases across the table, however, and we find that among those scored highest (*3*) on the index, two-thirds made this choice.

This examination, then, substantiates the validity of the composite index of scientific orientations. Faculty members designated as more or less scientific on the index appear, correspondingly, more or less scientific in their responses to the choice of faculty duties. Other items in the questionnaire provide a further validation of the index.

Table 4 presents the relationships between the composite index and responses to the other two items discussed earlier in this chapter: lecture preferences and preferences for faculty member training. Line (*a*) of the table shows that as scores on the index increase, so do faculty preferences for the scientific lectures: from 34 to 65 percent. The effect of the index is even stronger with regard to faculty preferences for research experience as the best training for their colleagues. Of those scored lowest (*0*) on the index, 43 percent favored research experience, while 89 percent of those scored highest (*3*) expressed this preference.

TABLE 4

FURTHER VALIDATION OF THE SCIENTIFIC-ORIENTATION INDEX

	Index of Scientific Orientations			
	Low 0	*1*	*2*	High 3
(*a*) Percentage interested in attending scientific* lectures	34 (38)†	42 (106)	46 (132)	65 (107)
(*b*) Percentage who say the best faculty training is as a researcher‡	43 (46)	60 (112)	65 (144)	89 (114)

*Percentage who chose the topics "Lipid Metabolism" and "The Role of Serotonin in Disorders of the Gut."

† Number in parentheses represents number of cases on which percentage is based. The number of cases shown for a given index score varies from one item to another, owing to the failure of some respondents to answer each question.

‡ Percentage who chose "Experience as a medical researcher" or "Experience as a basic science investigator."

The findings presented in tables 3 and 4 offer confirmation of the belief that the composite index of scientific orientations is a sufficient measure for the purposes of the analysis to follow. The index scores assigned to faculty members offer a reasonable means for distinguishing the more science-oriented from the less science-oriented. Before proceeding, one important point ought to be stressed.

The index scores do not permit us to identify "scientists" and "nonscientists" in terms of any absolute standard. We may only conclude that faculty members with relatively high scores on the index are more scientifically oriented than those with lower scores. The terms "scientist" and "nonscientist" will be used occasionally for ease of reporting, but the reader must bear in mind that no absolute designation is either intended or warranted.

Orientations and Activities

The intent of the immediately preceding sections has been to measure *subjective* orientations to science among the sample of teaching physicians. In the next chapter we shall determine whether science-oriented faculty "think" like scientists when they deal with patients. To this end, we have measured the extent to which faculty are subjectively oriented to science.

Nothing in the composite index of scientific orientations per se bears on the extent to which faculty members actually participate in scientific research. Conceivably, a faculty member may have been scored as strongly oriented to science when in fact he does not participate in scientific research at all. On the whole, we should expect this to be unlikely, however.

This section analyzes the degree of correlation between scientific orientations and scientific activities. In part, it may be considered a further validation of the composite index; if there is no relationship between orientations and activities, we ought to reevaluate the meaning of the composite index. Ultimately, however, the findings to be presented show that when we speak of science-oriented faculty—in subjective terms—we shall also be speaking of those faculty who participate in scientific research.

An earlier discussion mentioned the vast expanse of research activities throughout American medical colleges. It should come as no surprise to discover that virtually all faculty members in the present survey report that they have engaged in research activities at some point in their careers. Indeed, 84 percent of the faculty said that they had engaged in research during the 1964–65 academic year. In addition, nearly half (45 percent) provided laboratory instruction to medical students, and 5 percent spent more than ten hours per week in that activity.

The types of research engaged in by faculty members vary. In the questionnaire, faculty members were presented with the list shown in table 5 and were asked to indicate all the research areas in which they had participated. Overall, the greatest concentration of research activities is found in the areas of subcellular, cellular, and organ processes research. These areas, of course, most typify the commonly accepted image of medical

TABLE 5

NUMBERS OF TEACHING PHYSICIANS WHO
HAVE ENGAGED IN RESEARCH

Research areas	Numbers who have done such research
Subcellular processes	124
Cellular processes	111
Organ and organ system processes	303
Epidemiology	94
Psychosomatic medicine	23
Medical education	116
Study of patients' total symptomatology and course of disease	222
Child development	41
Comprehensive child supervision	20
	Total = (439)*

* The total refers to the number of respondents who report research activities during their careers. The figures shown beside each research area add to a much higher number since many respondents checked more than one area.

research, with its laboratories, bell jars, and electron microscopes. This is clearly the kind of research the critics most often have in mind when they charge that medical science fosters a dissected and dehumanized view of patients.

At the same time, however, 222 faculty members have engaged in research aimed at understanding the totality of disease and patient care. Others report research in medical education and in psychosomatic medicine. The fewest numbers report research in comprehensive child supervision. These forms of "person" research clearly do not fit into the research syndrome which is frequently condemned for dehumanizing medicine. And, as we shall see shortly, medical school faculty members themselves make a distinction between "person" and "object" research.

Table 6 examines the relationship between subjective orientations to science and actual research activities. The first line

TABLE 6

SCIENTIFIC ORIENTATIONS AND RESEARCH ACTIVITIES

	Index of Scientific Orientations			
	Low 0	1	2	High 3
Percentage who				
(a) Have ever done research	94	94	97	100
(b) Did research during the 1964–65 academic year	61	76	94	99
(c) Have done "object" research*	54	75	96	95
(d) Are primarily interested in "object" research*	28	43	76	80
(e) Have done total symptomatology research	60	59	49	34
(f) Are primarily interested in total symptomatology research	26	26	12	3
100% =	(48)	(116)	(147)	(116)

Note: Number in parentheses represents number on which percentage is based.
* Research in subcellular, cellular, or organ and organ system processes.

of the table documents the fact that virtually all faculty have engaged in some kind of research at some time. Nevertheless, the likelihood of having done so is slightly lower among those scored low on the index of scientific orientations. Line (*b*) of the table presents a related finding. The most science-oriented faculty are the most likely to report having engaged in research during the academic year preceding the survey.

The remainder of the table examines the relationship between the index and different types of research. Line (*c*) indicates that science-oriented faculty were more likely to have engaged in some form of "object" research (subcellular, cellular, or organ and organ system processes). And when asked to state the areas of research which interested them the most, science-oriented faculty expressed a greater interest in "object" research problems. (See line (*d*).)

Lines (*e*) and (*f*) of table 6 tell the same story somewhat differently. In questioning faculty about their research activities, we were concerned to include all those activities which might legitimately be considered scientific research. It seemed important that the study not simply accept the common stereotype of medical research as being limited to laboratories and microscopes. To an extent, however, the sample of faculty members accept the stereotype themselves. While we might have expected the science-oriented to predominate in all areas of research, this is not the case.

Line (*e*) shows that increasing subjective scientific orientations, as measured by the index, actually decrease the likelihood of a faculty member ever having engaged in total symtomatology research. Those who are the least subjectively inclined to science were the most likely to have performed research of this kind. And line (*f*) shows they are more likely to *prefer* doing so.

These findings suggest, then, that faculty members themselves tend not to include "person" research in their general conception of what constitutes medical science. It might be argued, however, that two of the items in the index conflict substantively with participation in total symptomatology research. On the question regarding ultimate medical interests, for example, faculty interest in problems of total patient management was taken as an indication of no scientific orientation. Yet total symptomatology research would certainly require a concern about problems of total patient management. Similarly, total symptomatology research would clearly involve a greater concern for the effectiveness of treatments than would the several forms of "object" research.

The remaining item in the index does not share the apparent contamination inherent in the others, however. When faculty members were asked to identify their greatest teaching contribution as either practicing physicians or researchers, there is no reason to believe that total symptomatology researchers would be precluded from the latter identification. Nevertheless, they did not so identify themselves. This is most clearly seen when we reverse our normal direction of percentaging. One would expect that faculty members with a great deal of research experience (of any kind) would be more likely to say that they could make their greatest contribution as researchers. Among all those faculty members who have engaged in total symptomatology research, only 29 percent said they could best serve as researchers, while 43 percent of all those who have never done such research gave this response.[3]

3. This may also be seen when research interests are compared with responses to the question regarding the greatest teaching contribution the respondent could make. Faculty members primarily interested in total symptomatology research are less likely to see their greatest contributions as medical researchers than is true of those with more traditional research interests.

Primary Research Interest	Percent saying "researcher"
Subcellular research	46 (56)
Cellular research	44 (25)
Organ and organ system research	36 (176)
Total symptomatology	14 (57)

In short, faculty members are inclined not to believe that "person" research qualifies them for the identification as researchers. Rather, they accept the more common conceptualization of medical science as involving laboratories, microscopes, cells, and tissues. In the remainder of the analysis, we must bear in mind that this is the conceptualization which informed the faculty responses used in the construction of the subjective index of scientific orientations.

This is not to suggest that the various forms of "person" research which have been increasing on medical campuses are not scientific; surely the faculty members engaging in such research would be the first to deny such a suggestion. Nevertheless, the finding regarding "person" research and scientific identification is interesting descriptively, and—more important—it facilitates the remaining analyses which are concerned with the consequences of commitment to science in its more conventional sense. When we speak of "scientists" in the following pages and chapters, we shall be speaking of those faculty members who represent the conventional notions of "object" research. Those who are engaged in unconventional research—aimed at studying whole patients—will be designated nonscientists.

THE TREND TOWARD SCIENCE

A good deal has been said about the trend toward science in American medicine as a whole. Implicit in the charges directed against medical educators has been the belief that a similar trend may be found on medical college campuses.

The present cross-sectional survey of teaching physicians cannot provide trend data which would prove or disprove the existence of a general movement in the direction of science among medical educators. This could only be accomplished through the use of data collected at different points in time. Nevertheless, the present data do permit us to approximate such a test. To do this, we shall examine the relationships between scientific orientations, on the one hand, and age, era of medical training, and academic rank, on the other. Each of these items provides at least a tentative test of the possible trend toward science, among medical school faculty.

Age and Scientific Orientations

Before examining this first relationship, it is necessary to recognize that faculty members' ages represent two distinct variables. On the one hand, age represents maturity, experience, and particular life situations. At the same time, age also has a cohort implication. Unfortunately, these two aspects of age cannot be separated adequately in the present study, although we are exclusively concerned here with the cohort aspect.

The logic of the present examination is that the younger faculty are the wave of the future; the older faculty are the remnants of the past. If the younger faculty members are more science-oriented than their older colleagues, this will be taken as a tentative indication of a trend toward science. All the data reported earlier, pertaining to the medical profession as a whole, would suggest this will be the case.

TABLE 7

AGE AND SCIENTIFIC ORIENTATIONS

Age	Percentage Scientists*
35 or under	64 (114)
36 to 45	65 (204)
46 to 55	56 (87)
56 or over	41 (22)

Note: Number in parentheses represents number of cases on which percentage is based.

* In this and subsequent tables, faculty members who score 2 or 3 on the index of scientific orientations are designated "scientists."

Table 7 verifies the expected relationship, although it is not as strong as some readers might have expected. Among faculty thirty-five or under, 64 percent are designated as scientists (scores of *2* or *3* on the index). The percentage is essentially the same for those in the thirty-six to forty-five age group, but it drops off as we move to the two older groups. Only 41 percent of the faculty fifty-six or over are designated scientists.

The data, then, provide some support for the belief that succeeding generations of teaching physicians are increasingly scientific in their orientations. It bears repeating, however, that this conclusion must be regarded as tentative. Conceivably, most faculty members turn away from science as they become older. If this is the case, the young scientists in this sample might be expected to become less scientific as they grow older, thus denying any overall trend. While there is simply no way of testing this alternative possibility in the present analysis, it should be noted that the *apparent* trend among faculty members coincides with the more firmly substantiated trend toward science in American medicine generally.

Medical Era and Scientific Orientations

Essentially the same conclusions are to be drawn from the examination of scientific orientations and the eras in which the teaching physicians were trained. In the questionnaire, faculty members were asked to indicate the year in which they received their M.D. degrees. This information has been utilized in table 8 to examine the relationship between medical era and scientific orientations.

With one exception, the degree of scientific orientations appears to have increased with each succeeding generation of medical graduates in the sample. The twenty-five faculty members who graduated during the 1960s provide the single exception; indeed, they are the least scientific of all. This finding somewhat corresponds to the finding in table 7 that showed the

TABLE 8

ERA OF MEDICAL TRAINING AND SCIENTIFIC ORIENTATIONS

Date M.D. degree received	Percentage Scientists
Prior to 1940	44 (43)
1940 to 1949	62 (133)
1950 to 1959	67 (221)
1960 or later	36 (25)

Note: Number in parentheses represents number of cases on which percentage is based.

youngest group to be no more scientific than the next older group.

In addition to substantiating, at least tentatively, the overall trend toward science among medical faculty members, the two preceding tables also suggest that the trend is more complicated than might be imagined. The two exceptions noted above suggest that new, young faculty members may increase somewhat in their scientific orientations during their early professional years. This possibility is further elaborated when we turn to a consideration of academic rank.

Academic Rank and Scientific Orientations

Given the overall relationships between scientific orientations, on the one hand, and age and era of medical training,

TABLE 9

ACADEMIC RANK AND SCIENTIFIC ORIENTATIONS

Academic Rank	Percentage Scientists
Instructor	59 (64)
Assistant professor	62 (154)
Associate professor	71 (105)
Professor	54 (100)

Note: Number in parentheses represents number of cases on which percentage is based.

on the other, we should expect that the lower academic ranks would contain considerably higher proportions of scientists than the senior ranks. This is not true, however, as table 9 shows.

Except for the full professors, who are the least science-oriented, the relationship between rank and science is just the opposite of what might have been expected. As we move from instructor through assistant professor to associate professor, we note a significant *increase* in scientific orientations. This, then, directly contradicts the previous findings with regard to age and era of training.

As one would imagine, the correlations among age, rank, and era of training are very high, but they are not perfect. The disparity between age and rank, particularly, permits a more careful examination of the foregoing, contradictory findings.

TABLE 10

AGE, RANK, AND SCIENTIFIC ORIENTATIONS

	Percentage Scientists			
Rank	Age			
	35 or under	36 to 45	46 to 55	56 or over
Instructor	57 (44)	59 (17)	* (3)	†
Assistant professor	69 (65)	56 (85)	* (4)	†
Associate professor	* (3)	73 (75)	63 (24)	* (3)
Professor	†	69 (26)	52 (56)	41 (71)

Note: Number in parentheses represents number of cases on which percentage is based.
* Too few cases for a stable percentage.
† No cases in this cell.

Table 10, therefore, presents the simultaneous relationships among age, rank, and scientific orientations.

While the findings are not altogether consistent, two conclusions are warranted. In the three senior academic ranks, scientific orientations decrease with age much more consistently than was found in table 7. Only among the instructors— including only the two youngest age groups—is this not the case.

And when we examine the relationship between rank and science within age groups, we note that the previously observed, positive relationship only pertains to the two youngest age groups. Among faculty thirty-five or under, the move from instructor to assistant professor coincides with a significant increase in scientific orientations. Among faculty thirty-six to forty-five, there is a general increase in scientific orientations with increasing rank—comparing the two junior ranks with the two senior ranks. Among the older faculty, however, the meager, available evidence suggests that the opposite is true.

These latest findings are more suggestive than conclusive. What they suggest, however, is that although scientific orientations generally decrease with age, the young, junior faculty members do not begin their teaching careers with an especially strong scientific orientation. There appears to be a tendency for their orientations to move more in the direction of science during their early faculty years, however, and this is especially true of those who move rapidly up the academic ladder. Whether their promotions make them more scientific or whether scientists are promoted faster than nonscientists cannot, of course, be determined from those data.

At the very least, these findings should serve as a clue to a much more complex process relating scientific orientations to age, rank, and era of medical training. While there is some evidence of a trend toward science among medical faculty members, it is more ambiguous than was first imagined.

SUMMARY

This chapter has laid the groundwork for the subsequent analyses in the book. We began with a general overview of scientific orientations among the sample of teaching physicians. By presenting faculty responses to several questions which juxtaposed concerns for scientific issues with the more traditional concerns for patient care, it was intended that readers might gain a better understanding of the general pattern of interests among medical educators. As mentioned earlier, there is no absolute standard by which to judge whether these faculty responses represent too much or too little science in their professional perspectives. Each reader must decide for himself.

The main task of this chapter has been to create a single measure of scientific orientations which will permit later analyses of the consequences of science in medicine. To gauge the effects of science, it is necessary to distinguish scientists from nonscientists among the sample of faculty members. Three questionnaire items were found especially suitable to the construction of a composite index of scientific orientations. Taken at face value, each appeared to reflect the kind of scientific orientation which critics of contemporary medicine so often decry. Moreover, the simultaneous interrelations of responses to the three items confirmed the belief that they all reflected a common dimension. The three items were used to create a composite index of scientific orientations. This index proved to be a powerful mechanism for predicting faculty responses to other questions which also reflected scientific orientations. In this manner, the index was validated.

Although the composite index was conceived and created as a measure of subjective orientations to science, the subsequent analysis showed that scores on the index were closely related to actual participation in scientific research as well. Thus when we later refer to faculty members who *think* like scientists, we shall be referring to those who *act* like scientists as well.

Finally, the composite index was used to examine the possible trend toward science among medical faculty members. In considering faculty members' ages and the eras in which they were trained, the findings pointed generally in the direction of an increase in scientific orientations over the years. The examination of academic ranks, however, suggested that the trend is much more complex than might otherwise be supposed. While inconclusive, the findings suggest that a more sophisticated examination is needed in future studies of this issue.

Having created a reasonable means for distinguishing scientists from nonscientists among the sample of medical faculty, we will now examine the impact of science on humane patient care. Are the scientists in the sample less compassionate, less responsible, and less respectful of medical patients than the nonscientists?

CHAPTER TWO

The Effects of Science on Care

The purpose of this chapter, and the central focus of part one, is to test the allegation that scientific emphases in contemporary American medicine undermine the traditional norms of humane patient care. It has been charged that physicians, and especially medical school faculty members, have increasingly focused their attention on scientific issues and that this has led to a loss of respect for the patient as a total human being. An earlier discussion presented the theoretical grounds for supposing that science might undermine humane patient care. It was concluded that there are sufficient reasons for the fear that scientifically oriented faculty members might be less compassionate in dealing with patients, less responsible for their patients' well-being, and generally less concerned over the value of human life.

The preceding chapter has shown the extent to which medical school faculty members are oriented to scientific issues as opposed to the traditional concerns of healing. Some faculty, indeed, appear wholly committed to science, while others express little or no interest in it. Although there is some evidence of a trend toward scientific orientations among medical school faculty members, it must be conceded that not all faculty have been affected. This finding, however, will hardly alleviate fears that medical care is being dehumanized by science.

For our purposes, the observed variation in faculty orientations permits a test of the allegation. The preceding chapter was devoted primarily to the creation of a measure of scientific orientations which would permit us to distinguish scientists from nonscientists among the sample of faculty members. We shall now use that measure in an empirical test of the propositions that the more scientific faculty members are less compassionate, less responsible for patients' well-being, and basically less respectful of human life. The question of compassion will be examined in the context of the university hospital ward. The question of responsibility will be examined in the same context. Both of these examinations will reflect indirectly on faculty members' respect for the human worth of patients; for a more direct examination, we shall consider faculty attitudes on the matter of human experimentation.

The analyses to be presented in this chapter provide our first examination of the interplay between medical science and medical morality. At this point, we are only concerned with medical morality in the context of patient-physician interaction. These first analyses deal only with the allegations directed against science with regard to humane patient-physician relations. Parts two and three will move beyond these concerns to consider medical morality in a broader, social context.

Scientific Orientations and Compassion

The humane physician is expected to treat his patients with compassion. He must be sensitive to the pathos which so frequently accompanies his professional efforts. While he cannot become so involved in the lives of his patients as to lose his facility for rational judgment, he cannot remain totally aloof, removed, and impersonal in his relations with his patients.

With increasing frequency, however, one hears that physicians, generally, exhibit the objective detachment in patient care which is more appropriate to medical research. Not surprisingly, this charge is most frequently directed against medical school faculty members—those who have the greatest general preoccupation with science.

Patricia Kendall has done extensive interviewing among physicians in university towns, and she reports:

Our informants pointed to various manifestations of the impersonality. Some reported that, because of their research-teaching orientation, medical educators are inclined to view patients as specimens of particular diseases, which makes impossible the development of a genuinely warm doctor-patient relationship. Other practitioners find the impersonality of academic medicine manifested in the medical needs and concerns of their patients; thus, quite a few suggested that practising physicians appreciate better than do medical educators the psychological needs and worries of their patients. They report that most of their patients prefer to be hospitalized in the local community hospitals which have a more informal and casual atmosphere.[1]

Science-oriented faculty members, therefore, are considered less sensitive to the human aspects of medicine. Since scientific activities are of necessity objective and detached—devoid of human compassion—it is believed that this dispassionate mode is carried over into the actual care of patients. Nor are the community practitioners alone in this belief. Indeed, Dr. Kendall seems to agree with them. Speaking of medical education, she says:

Such impersonality is sometimes attributed to other features of

1. Patricia Kendall, "The Relationship Between Medical Educators and Medical Practitioners," *Annals of the New York Academy of Sciences,* September 1965, p. 575.

modern medical education, such as the divided responsibility implicit in the hierarchical structure of a teaching hospital. For the sake of convenience, we treat it as a by-product of a growing research orientation.[2] . . . Educators seem unaware that the training programs they have developed, emphasizing research and a team approach, must almost inevitably lead to an impersonal attitude toward patients.[3]

George Reader is another who seems to perceive an inevitable link between science and impersonality. Although he notes that "Scientific investigation is inseparable from good practice; each contributes to the other,"[4] he is concerned that an emphasis on science detracts from personalized care. "Perhaps a heavier science requirement for admission [to medical school] will help produce better medical scientists, but will it also ensure a supply of physicians interested in their patients as people?"[5]

Comments such as these, then, suggest that medical science is responsible for depersonalization in contemporary medicine. Medical scientists are alleged to be more detached in their care of patients than are less scientific practicing physicians. And the emphasis on science is said to encourage a depersonalized view of patients among medical students. Other, less sophisticated observers have simply equated science and impersonality.

The compassion expected of the physician is not limited to his dealings with patients. Often his professional duties bring him in contact with the anxieties and, perhaps, grief of his pa-

2. Patricia Kendall, *The Relationship Between Medical Educators and Medical Practitioners* (Evanston, Ill.: Association of American Medical Colleges, 1962), p. 165.
3. *Ibid.*, p. 167.
4. George Reader, M.D., "Contributions of Sociology to Medicine," in *Handbook of Medical Sociology*, ed. Howard F. Freeman, et al. (Englewood Cliffs, N.J.: Prentice-Hall, 1963), p. 2.
5. *Ibid.*, p. 7.

tient's family. The physician's compassion and consideration for the patient's family has been commented upon by one of Kendall's informants. A general practitioner criticized medical faculty members, saying:

> For instance, supposing your mother is being operated on. The professor finishes the operation, and he goes on to the next thing on his schedule. He doesn't take time to come down to the room and say, "Mary, your mother's operation was a success. There was no malignancy. She's upstairs in the recovery room now, and she'll be there for a couple of hours more." I'm the one to do that. I never leave the operating room without going downstairs to see the patient's relatives.[6]

Clearly, this community physician is stressing the need for a degree of compassion on the part of the physician. What he decries is the detachment with which the "professor" moves along to the next item on his schedule without considering the anxieties of his patient's family.

Faculty members in the present study were presented with the following situation. "Suppose you were the attending physician for a non-private ward patient who had died. Would you personally speak to the surviving family, or would you delegate this duty to the house staff?" The preceding comments regarding the supposed detachment of science-oriented faculty members would lead one to expect that they would be the most likely to delegate the duty—not caring to involve themselves personally in the emotionally charged confrontation with the grief-stricken family. Nonscientists, on the other hand, might be expected to exhibit greater compassion in this regard. Table 11 presents faculty responses, arranged according to scientific orientations.

The majority of all faculty members say they would nor-

6. Kendall (AAMC monograph), *Medical Educators and Practitioners*, p. 168.

TABLE 11

RESPONSES TO PATIENT'S DEATH—BY SCIENTIFIC ORIENTATIONS

Question: Would you personally speak to the surviving family, or would you delegate this duty to the house staff?	Index of Scientific Orientations				
	Low 0	1	2	High 3	Total
In almost every instance, would speak to them personally	9%	14%	12%	19%	14%
Generally speak to them, but would occasionally delegate the duty	26	15	20	15	17
Generally delegate but would occasionally speak to them personally	46	62	61	54	58
In almost every instance would delegate the duty	19	9	7	12	11
100% =	(47)	(116)	(147)	(116)	(452)

Note: Number in parentheses represents number of cases on which percentage is based.

mally delegate the duty to the house staff.[7] Modally, they say, "As a general rule, I would delegate this duty to the house staff, although I might occasionally speak to the surviving family personally." Roughly a third of the faculty members said they would personally speak to the family, at least as a general rule.

In their responses to this question, the most scientific faculty members seem every bit as compassionate as the nonscientific faculty. If anything, scientific faculty appear slightly more compassionate. We note that 19 percent of those faculty scored highest (3) on the index say they would almost always speak to the surviving family, as compared with only 9 percent of

7. This finding may come as a shock to some readers. It should be noted that the question involved a "non-private ward patient"—that is, one assigned to the physician as part of his university duties. One would expect a different response from faculty members if a private patient were involved. However, this qualification may not satisfy the sensibilities of many readers.

those scored lowest (0). When the first two responses are combined, however, we find both groups about equally disposed to speaking to the family at least as a general rule.

Ultimately, the safest conclusion to be drawn from this table is that scientific orientations are irrelevant to compassion in patient care. While some faculty appear more compassionate than others, science does not seem to be the determining factor. Thus, this first test of the allegation that science undermines humane patient care disconfirms the common expectation.

It should be admitted that this single indicator of compassion is less than ideal. Nevertheless, if scientific orientations truly undermine feelings of compassion, as is so often suggested, that effect should have been somewhat apparent in the present instance. That no effect was discovered weakens the general allegation regarding science and humane patient care. The following analyses will add to the weight of evidence in that regard.

Scientific Orientations and Responsibility for Patients

The humane physician is expected to accept a fiduciary responsibility for the welfare of his patient. This means that the physician acts on behalf of his patient; his patient's interests become his own. Ultimately, his commitment to playing this role conscientiously should be as strong as if the physician were acting in his own behalf. While the physician is not expected to be successful in all his professional efforts, he must do everything in his power to aid his patient. The patient, on his part, admits he cannot heal himself and places his trust in the physician's sense of personal responsibility.

It has been suggested frequently that science-oriented faculty members do not take their fiduciary responsibility for patients as seriously as they should. The nature of the suggestions varies, but the common denominator is that such men are so wrapped up in scientific concerns and activities that they play down the ultimate significance of healing as such. Once again, the extensive interviewing of physicians by Patricia Kendall illustrates this criticism.

To begin with, it is said that, as the faculty becomes increasingly absorbed in its research activities, it becomes correspondingly less interested in the practice of medicine. Some practitioners see this as interfering with the humane treatment of patients. A few became almost irate in their interviews when they recalled instances in which, for example, a hospitalized patient was denied a rare drug so that experiments using the drug would not have to be interrupted until the supply could be replenished.[8]

By and large, the alleged crime of irresponsibility in medicine is one of omission rather than commission. The charge that science-oriented physicians do the wrong things to patients is less frequently made than the charge that they fail to dedicate themselves seriously to doing the right things. Thus, patients may fear that a science-oriented physician will not pay sufficient attention to their needs, that they will interest him only to the extent that they represent an engaging scientific problem.

In the context of medical education, the alleged association between scientific orientations and irresponsible patient care is frequently couched in a concern for the future of American medicine. As in the case of alleged detachment, it is feared that medical students will take on the same orientations exhibited by their instructors. Another of Kendall's informants expressed this concern in criticizing medical school faculty members.

They forget they're supposed to turn out practitioners. One of the first things I noticed when I got down here was the interns at the Medical Center don't take responsibility for patients as they should. For a long time I tried to figure out the reason for this.

8. Kendall (*Annals* article), "Relationship Between Educators and Practitioners," p. 574.

Finally, I realized it's because they never see professors taking care of patients. Doctors learn by imitation, and if they don't have someone to imitate, they won't learn. *Because they didn't see any of their professors treating patients, they didn't develop an appropriate sense of responsibility for patients.*[9]

Most faculty members in the clinical departments of Medicine and Pediatrics are assigned the task of attending university patients. Some report caring for more than a hundred such patients during the course of the 1964–65 academic year. At the same time, however, these same faculty have teaching duties, and many also conduct research activities, as noted earlier. It becomes apparent when these facts are considered that the role of attending physician in the university hospital differs greatly from the more traditional attending role associated with the family physician in private practice.

For present purposes, the most salient difference is found in the faculty member's reliance on the assistance of hospital personnel in caring for the patients assigned him. This is brought about by the possible incompatibility of his patient load and other duties, plus the presence of a large and varied professional support staff. If he serves in a large university hospital, the faculty member may find nurses, interns, specialists, psychiatrists, social workers, dieticians, ministers, and medical students participating in the care of his patients.

It is rather simple to imagine the ways in which a faculty attending physician might evade his responsibility to his patients. Like most bureaucracies, the house staff of the university hospital is capable of functioning effectively without direct supervision—at least for a period of time. Like many bureaucratic administrators, then, the faculty attending physician may often find his patients being cared for reasonably well even when he himself takes no active role in the process.

9. Kendall (AAMC monograph), *Medical Educators and Practitioners*, p. 155.

With others around to perform the specific day-to-day tasks, he might be tempted to devote his main attentions elsewhere and trust to the proficiency of the house staff. Such a course of action, however, would represent a violation of the personal responsibility expected of an attending physician. And, of course, it is precisely this which is alleged to be the typical reaction of science-oriented faculty members in university hospitals.

We shall turn now to an empirical examination of the allegation's validity. The data available for this part of the analysis concern the behavior of faculty members in their duties as attending physicians for non-private ward patients assigned them in the university hospital. As a result, the examination must be limited to those faculty who were assigned patients during the 1964–65 academic year. It should be noted, however, that over three-fourths of the faculty members in the study were assigned hospital patients and that scientific orientations were not related to the fact or the extent of such assignments.[10] Thus, while some faculty members will be omitted from this examination, the omission is necessary and does not seem a serious one.

Granting that a faculty member must rely on the house staff to some extent, one important demonstration of a personal sense of responsibility would be found in his supervision of those assisting him. To examine this issue, faculty members were asked about the manner in which they supervised the house staff. "What was the procedure by which the house staff reported to you on the care of the staff patients assigned to you as attending physician?" The questionnaire offered three alternatives regarding ways in which the house staff reported: "daily at a specified time," "informally nearly every

10. The methodological notes in Appendix A present tables showing that the index of scientific orientations is not related to (a) serving as an attending physician on a non-private ward service, (b) the number of months spent in such service, or (c) the number of patients served.

day," and "only when particular circumstances required your attention."

The assumption implicit in this question was that the closeness of supervision exhibited by faculty members was an indication of the degree of their personal responsibility in the care of patients. Thus, requiring the house staff to report daily at a specified time would indicate the greatest sense of responsibility, while requiring reports only when circumstances warranted them seemed to indicate the weakest sense of personal responsibility. (In response to this question, several faculty members wrote in the answer "three times a week," so this response has been included among those reported in table 12.)

TABLE 12

HOUSE STAFF SUPERVISION—BY SCIENTIFIC ORIENTATIONS

Question: How often did house staff report?	Index of Scientific Orientations				
	Low			High	
	0	1	2	3	Total
Daily at a specified time	57%	59%	58%	55%	57%
Informally nearly every day	13	23	22	18	20
Three times a week*	3	6	6	4	6
When circumstances required	27	12	14	23	17
100% =	(30)	(80)	(103)	(66)	(293)

Note: Number in parentheses represents number of cases on which percentage is based.

* This response was not provided in the questionnaire, but many faculty members wrote it in.

Overall, more than half the faculty members chose the answer reflecting the closest supervision of the house staff: daily reports at specified times. Yet, as the table also indicates, scientists and nonscientists did not differ in this regard. Virtually identical proportions indicated the highest degree of personal responsibility, and the remaining responses also support the conclusion that there is no consistent relationship between scientific orientations and patient responsibility.

Another question in the questionnaire was designed to measure faculty members' exercise of personal responsibility for their university hospital patients. This question was also based on a recognition that attending physicians in the university hospital have a finite amount of time to devote to patient care. Given that faculty attending physicians could not always be on duty when their patients required care, we asked: "During your 'off-duty' hours, what was the *normal* procedure for making major diagnostic and therapeutic decisions regarding the staff patients assigned to you as attending physician?"

In this instance, faculty members were given two options for delegating the responsibility to others (members of the house staff or "on-duty" faculty made the decisions) and one which would indicate their retention of personal responsibility ("I was called to make these decisions"). Four out of ten faculty members reported that they themselves had normally been called in to make the major decisions relating to the patients assigned to them. Yet, as table 13 shows, this response is not related to their scientific orientations.

TABLE 13

OFF-DUTY DECISIONS—BY SCIENTIFIC ORIENTATIONS

Question: During off-duty hours, who made major decisions regarding your patients?	Index of Scientific Orientations				
	Low			High	
	0	1	2	3	Total
Members of the house staff	42%	42%	57%	49%	50% ⎤
"On-duty" faculty members	25	12	4	12	10
I was called to make them	33	46	39	39	40
100% =	(24)	(78)	(96)	(77)	(292)

Note: Number in parentheses represents number of cases on which percentage is based.

Scientific and nonscientific faculty members do not differ significantly in maintaining personal responsibility for their patients or in delegating that responsibility to others. The allegation that medical scientists are less responsible in the care of patients simply does not hold up under empirical examination.

The conclusion to be drawn from these latest two tables coincides with the earlier conclusion regarding science and compassion. Scientific orientations among teaching physicians do not, in and of themselves, undermine the traditional norms of compassion and responsibility which have been associated with humane patient care in American medicine. Some faculty members, to be sure, appear more committed to the traditional norms than are others, but whether or not they are strongly oriented to science is irrelevant. On the basis of the available evidence, then, we must conclude that the trend toward science in American medicine does not constitute a threat to humane patient care.

The next section examines faculty attitudes regarding human experimentation. In that examination, we shall be concerned to discover whether scientific orientations do diminish faculty members' basic respect for the value of human life.

Scientific Orientations and Human Experimentation

The humane physician is expected to respect his patient's intrinsic identity as a fellow human being. In this regard, we speak of patients as persons rather than objects. Human life is regarded as far more sacred than material objects. Through compassion and responsibility, the practicing physician gives evidence of recognizing and respecting the worth of human life. And it is contended that dispassionate and irresponsible physicians have no respect for human life.

As much as this issue is debated and discussed within the context of patient care, it comes most directly to a head in human experimentation in connection with medical research. In the search for more effective preventive and therapeutic techniques, it has become increasingly inappropriate to study only animals and human cadavers. To determine the effects of medical treatments on living persons, it is, in fact, necessary to experiment on living persons.

A. C. Ivy attests to the necessity for such research, and also points out that medical research must be seen in broadly defined terms.

In the medical sciences, the only method which can clearly reveal and establish the cause, prevention, and treatment of disease is the method of controlled experimentation on animals and volunteer human subjects. Even after the therapy of a disease is discovered, its application to the patient remains in part experimental. Because of the physiological variations in the response of different patients to the same therapy, the therapy of disease is, and always will be, an experimental aspect of medicine.[11]

The experimental nature of medical care is even clearer when one examines the drug-testing procedures which exist in the United States. The recent thalidomide alarm brought this latter issue to the attention of many laymen. (See chapter six.)

The developments of new surgical techniques must also be viewed as medical experiments. In seeking the earliest legal precedents regarding human experimentation, scholars generally agree on the malpractice suit brought in 1767 against a prominent English surgeon who attempted to rebreak a badly mended fracture. What is now accepted as a legitimate procedure was then viewed as human experimentation and condemned.[12]

11. A. C. Ivy, "The History and Ethics of the Use of Human Subjects in Medical Experiments," in *Clinical Investigation in Medicine: Legal, Ethical, and Moral Aspects,* eds. Irving Ladimer and Roger W. Newman (Boston: Boston University, Law-Medicine Research Institute, 1963), p. 39. (Emphasis in the original.)
12. Sister v. Baker, 1767; see Irving Ladimer, "Ethical and Legal Aspects of Medical Research on Human Beings," *ibid.,* p. 182.

Just as many medical treatments may be viewed as experiments, there are those who would contend that all medical practice might be viewed as medical research. Martini and Shimkin discuss diagnosis, prescription, clinical observation, and record-keeping in terms of hypothesis formation and testing.[13] It is important to recognize the significance of such "passive" or "natural" experiments, since they often provide the basis upon which many new techniques are initially devised. As Henry K. Beecher has pointed out: "Nature presents us with bolder experiments than we could ever dare to perform ourselves. We profit from a study of them, *basic* science profits.[14]

Nevertheless, it is also essential to distinguish between experiments which are inherent in a patient's care and those which do not relate directly to the efforts to heal him. While this line is sometimes a fine one to draw, the major moral questions regarding human experimentation involve situations in which the patient-subject does not stand to benefit directly from the experiment itself. And the issues are sharpest when he is actually endangered by the experiment.

Experiments of this sort are conducted every day in medical research. The danger involved varies from experiment to experiment, and subjects risk that danger without the likelihood that their own health will improve directly from the experimental treatment. As a good example, the field of space medicine has faced the necessity of determining human endurance with regard to pressure, temperature, altitude, gravity, isolation, and a host of other environmental variables. In order to safeguard the lives of present and future spacemen, it has been obligatory to document their needs and their natural

13. Paul Martini, "Experimental Design in Clinical Medicine," and Michael B. Shimkin, "The Problem of Experimentation on Human Beings: The Research Worker's Point of View," *ibid.*
14. Henry K. Beecher, *Experimentation in Man* (Springfield, Ill.: Charles C Thomas, 1958), p. 3.

adaptability. Hence, men and women who may never walk in space have undertaken discomfort and danger to permit the advancement of medical science.

Of course, the most nightmarish example of such experimentation took place in the Nazi concentration camps of Auschwitz, Dachau, and Buchenwald. Political prisoners were involuntarily subjected to inhumane and often deadly experiments which held no hope of benefit for them personally. No doubt this bizarre miscarriage of science has been the single most important source of subsequent concern about the ethics of human experimentation.

It is hardly surprising to find that a number of official and semiofficial codes have been developed and published to deal with this situation. The contemporary codes seem to agree on the general principles that should inform the issue of risks in human experimentation. The main points are as follows: (a) whenever a possibility of danger exists, animals should be used as experimental subjects if feasible, and animals should always be used in the exploratory development of the experiment; (b) risks should be minimized wherever and to whatever extent possible; (c) no one should be forced or tricked into participating as a subject; and (d) the risks involved must be commensurate with the benefits to be gained. These several principles are succinctly stated in four of the principles drawn up by the Nuremberg Military Tribunals in 1947.[15]

Nuremberg Rule 1: The voluntary consent of the human subject is absolutely essential. *Rule 2:* The experiment should be such as to yield fruitful results for the good of society, unprocurable by other methods or means of study, and not random and unnecessary in nature. *Rule 3:* The experiment should be so designed and based on the results of animal experimentation and a knowledge of the natural history of the disease or other problem under study that the anticipated re-

15. Quoted in *ibid.,* pp. 51, 59, 60.

sults will justify the performance of the experiment. *Rule 6:*
The degree of risk to be taken should never exceed that determined by the humanitarian importance of the problem to
be solved by the experiment.

Of these several issues, perhaps the one most often discussed today concerns *who* should be a subject in the experiment. The first Nuremberg rule states explicitly that only
volunteers may be used, and there seems to be consensus on
this general rule today. (This, of course, was the most un-
conscionable crime committed by the Nazi experimenters.)[16]
Despite the consensus that seems to exist at a general level,
however, there is still a good deal of disagreement as to its
particulars. For example, many argue that medical students
and convicts cannot be considered volunteers. Despite a researcher's proclamations to the contrary, there is always a
strong likelihood that these captive groups will feel obliged
to participate—in hope of special rewards or in fear of negative sanctions.

In this analysis, we shall consider another aspect of the
question regarding who should participate in dangerous experiments. A number of observers have suggested that the
experimenter himself is obligated to undertake the same risks
he would ask of others. Henry Beecher says: "Experimentation
on other men requires a *willingness* to experiment upon one-
self as evidence of good faith." [17] Medical history provides
many examples of researchers following this principle. In re-

16. It is important to recognize this. While many of the Nazi experiments
   were indeed cruel and involved immense suffering as well as death, the
   humanitarian importance of some of the research problems with relation
   to the research dangers is attested to by contemporary medical research
   devoted to the same problems and involving many of the same risks. Nor
   is it wholly sufficient to condemn the Nazi experimenters as incompetent scientists, for much of the research is still quoted today. The primary Nazi crime lay in the involuntary selection of experimental
   subjects.
17. Beecher, *Experimentation,* p. 7.

cent times, Ivy personally participated in high-altitude flights to study the bends; both Salk and Sabin took their own polio vaccines.[18]

There is clearly another side to the issue, however. One might very well argue that the researcher who risks his life by participating in dangerous experiments is also risking his potential service to mankind. According to this point of view, the experimenter's courage constitutes a form of professional irresponsibility.

These two opposing viewpoints were expressed recently in regard to a series of experiments conducted by the Sloan-Kettering Institute for Cancer Research. Chester M. Southam and his colleagues were engaged in studies on resistance to cancer. During the course of their experiments, they implanted live cancer cells in human beings. In the beginning, cancer patients were used for the experiments, and the initial controversy was sparked by the researchers' frequent failure to obtain informed consent from the patients. In several cases, patients were told only that they would receive an injection of cells; they were not told about the nature of these cells.

Later in the research project, the cancer cells were injected into healthy volunteers at an Ohio prison. With regard to these latter experiments, the question was raised as to whether the experimenters themselves should not have participated as subjects. Elinor Langer quotes Dr. Southam, head of the project: "I would not have hesitated . . . if it would have served a useful purpose. But . . . to me it seemed like false heroism. . . . Let's face it, there are relatively few skilled cancer researchers, and it seemed stupid to take even the little risk." [19]

In response to Southam, Otto Guttentag suggested that the

18. Reported by Otto E. Guttentag in a letter on "Human Experimentation" in the August 21, 1964, issue of *Science,* p. 768.
19. Quoted in Elinor Langer, "Human Experimentation: Cancer Studies at Sloan-Kettering Stir Public Debate on Medical Ethics," *Science,* February 7, 1964, p. 551.

failure of the experimenter to participate in a dangerous experiment implies "a difference between the value of his existence and that of his fellow beings. . . . The 'false heroism' and the 'stupidity' of physicians who subject themselves to their experiments are manifestations of a more profound insight into the nature of the experimenter-subject relation in medical research and of the place of scientific endeavour in our culture than is the rationalism that the New York investigators invoke." [20] In this context, Guttentag pointed to the differences between medical research and other forms of scientific endeavor, stressing many of the ethical considerations discussed earlier.

Since human experimentation, and the question of experimenter participation, is such an important issue in the contemporary debate over research ethics, the medical school survey attempted to determine faculty attitudes in this regard. Teaching physicians in the study were presented with the following item in the questionnaire.

In the development of medical science, if it is deemed necessary to subject a group of healthy volunteers to a potentially dangerous experiment, do you feel the experimenter himself should or should not participate as an experimental subject? (Assume he is a suitable experimental subject.)

_____ I feel he has a *moral obligation* to participate
_____ I feel it is *generally unwise* for him to participate
_____ I feel he should be *prohibited* from participating
_____ Other (please specify)

The overall faculty response to this item is perhaps interesting in itself. About one faculty member in four selected the first response, saying the experimenter has a moral obligation to participate in his own dangerous experiment. Over half felt it was generally unwise for him to do so. At the same time, only 8 percent would prohibit him from participating.

20. Guttentag's letter in *Science*, August 21, 1964, p. 768.

Indicative of the complications of this issue is the fact that many faculty members were unwilling to select one of the responses offered, choosing to write in their own instead. Six percent said that the experimenter himself should decide whether to participate. Another 3 percent said he should be willing to do so, although they would not force participation upon him. Finally, 5 percent said they objected to the kind of experiment described in the question.

The purpose in asking this question, however, was to determine whether science-oriented faculty members would be less likely to support the experimenter's obligation to participate. The general allegations directed against medical science would suggest that the scientists among the sample would be the least likely to choose the first response. Table 14 shows that this allegation is not well-founded.

TABLE 14

PARTICIPATION IN EXPERIMENTS—BY SCIENTIFIC ORIENTATIONS

Question: Should an experimenter participate as a subject in his own experiments?	Index of Scientific Orientations				
	Low 0	1	2	High 3	Total
He has a *moral obligation* to participate	20%	25%	25%	25%	24%
It is *generally unwise* for him to participate	46	55	56	51	54
He should be *prohibited* from participating	17	6	3	14	8
Experimenter should decide*	10	6	7	6	6
He should be willing*	2	5	3	1	3
Should not experiment on human subjects*	5	4	6	4	5
100% =	(41)	(107)	(138)	(102)	(408)

Note: Number in parentheses represents number of cases on which percentage is based.

* These responses were not provided in the questionnaire, but were volunteered by several faculty members. Another 41 faculty members wrote in their own answers, but these could not be combined into any more general categories.

Once again, the scientists and nonscientists in the sample are more alike than different. The least science-oriented faculty are the least likely to support the experimenter's moral obligation to participate, but the difference is slight. Although other variations may be found in the table, none support the conclusion that scientists are less committed to the value of human life than are the nonscientists. Scientific orientations have no more effect on responses to this item than what was discovered with regard to compassion and responsibility.

Humane Medicine Reconsidered

The preceding analyses provide a consistent disconfirmation of the allegation that science undermines humane patient care. Scientific faculty members do not appear any less compassionate, less responsible, or less respectful of human life than those faculty with little or no commitment to medical science as such. Though the reader may question the validity of any or all of the present indicators of humane medical orientations,[21] the consistency of findings has generated a weight of evidence which cannot be dismissed.

The findings of this chapter require some additional comments, although the present medical faculty data do not permit an empirical elaboration of them. The primary reason why the common allegations directed against science are not supported by the present data lies, I believe, in a basic distinction between *cognitive* and *affective* modes: orientations of the head and heart, respectively.

As a cognitive mode, scientific orientations among medical school faculty members represent a certain hardheadedness or

21. The methodological notes contained in Appendix A show that the several indicators of humane medical care are related to one another. Although the items are not suitable to the construction of a composite index, their interrelations support the belief that each measures the same thing: faculty members' commitments to the traditional norms of humane care.

tough-mindedness. From this perspective, the highest premiums are on rigorous logic, empirical documentation, and analytical concerns. The hardheaded scientist demands facts in the place of intuition or feelings. It is the quality of tough-mindedness or hardheadedness, I think, which distinguishes science from humanism.

The danger, however, lies in equating hardheadedness with hardheartedness: confusing cognitive and affective modes. The equating of these two modes seems to lie at the base of the common allegations directed against science.[22] The analysis of this chapter has suggested, however, that cognitive and affective modes are not necessarily related.

If compassion, for example, may be taken as an indication of softheartedness among medical faculty members, we have seen that the hardheaded faculty (scientists) are as softhearted as anyone else in the study. Hardheadedness in this respect, then, is not related to hardheartedness.

Part one of this book has attempted to discover the relationship between medical science and medical morality. To that end, we have examined the possible effects of scientific orientations on several expressions of traditional medical morality. Within the context of patient-physician relations, we must conclude that medical science does not constitute a threat to traditional medical morality.

The more general conclusion one is tempted to draw from these findings is that medical science and medical morality are altogether irrelevant to one another. As pointed out in an earlier discussion, science is, ideally, amoral. Science is con-

22. In part, perhaps, this equation is related to the tools of the scientist's trade. The scientist is interested in hard facts, and facts most often imply measurement; measurement, in turn, requires measuring instruments. Thus the medical scientist may place a great deal of emphasis on the information he obtains from an electroencephalograph, an X ray, a microscope, and so forth. The nonscientist, on the other hand, may forgo the use of such instruments in favor of personal interrogation of the patient.

cerned solely with what *is,* not with what *ought to be.* This more general conclusion, however, flies in the face of a long history of conflicts between science and morality. For centuries, millennia even, science has challenged traditional moral perspectives and moral systems. And medical science has been no exception.

In the preceding analyses, we have taken a very narrow view of the relationship between medical science and medical morality. To fully grasp the interactions, we must now move to a more general level. We noted earlier that medical morality is based on a more general, social morality: a more general view of humane relations among men. In part two, which follows, we shall examine the relationship between scientific orientations and this more general social morality. In so doing, we shall gain a better understanding of the effects of medical science on specifically medical morality.

PART TWO

Science and Social Morality

INTRODUCTION TO PART TWO

Many readers will no doubt find it difficult to accept the findings of the preceding analyses. Too much has been written, too many anecdotes recounted, to give up easily the belief that medical science undermines the traditional norms of humane patient-physician relations. Probably all of us know of someone who has had to suffer under the care of a physician who seemed unconcerned about his patient's well-being, interested only in the scientific aspects of the patient's case. Nevertheless, the findings of part one indicate that for every uncaring, scientific physician, there is another uncaring, *nonscientific* physician. Science per se does not make physicians detached and unconcerned. At the same time, this conclusion represents only part of the picture.

Part two of this book advances the thesis that science is indeed undermining traditional morality. However, the phenomenon which we shall examine is much more general and more significant than might be imagined. Medical science is part of the general movement which is undermining a basic morality of American society as a whole. This movement is, of course, relevant to medical morality, but it is not limited to medicine alone.

In brief overview, the thesis to be advanced is the following. In the past, American society, including American medicine, has been informed by a morality of individual responsibility. Each individual has been held accountable for his own actions and for his success or failure in life. This individualistic morality, in turn, has been based on a belief in man's ultimate freedom. It has been believed that each person possessed the ultimate freedom for shaping his own destiny. Both the individualistic morality and the image of man as a free-will agent have had their roots in Christian religiosity and political conservatism.

The scientific perspective, however, suggests a radically different image of man: as being largely determined by environmental and biological forces over which he has little or no control. This deterministic image of man is virtually a requirement of Western science. As a result, scientific perspectives conflict with the perspectives of Christian religiosity and political conservatism. Moreover, the decline of the latter perspectives has coincided with the growth of science. Ultimately, we are witnessing a decline in the traditional, individualistic morality and its replacement by a more deterministic social morality. This latter development has implications for medical morality and for all of American society.

The Traditional "Individualistic" Morality

The introduction to part one pointed to the importance of the individual in American history. Traditionally, American morality has been based on a belief in individual responsibility for behavior. This perspective has been evident in most of our social institutions. American religion has emphasized the individual's accountability before his God. American law holds the individual responsible (hence punishable) for antisocial behavior. And our capitalistic economic institutions have been based on the individual's responsibility for his behavior in the marketplace.

These moral judgments, holding the individual responsible for his behavior, are based on a belief in individual freedom. American institutions and American values have been grounded in the implicit, ontological belief that man is ultimately free, that freedom is his natural state.

From this perspective, then, one explains human behavior in terms of qualities to be found (or imputed) in the total human actor. If one wishes to explain why John Smith rose from his humble position as son of a bootblack to become president of a large corporation, one must look into John Smith's total being—his personality, his willpower, his inner strength—for the answer. And, correspondingly, the son of a corporation president who falls to the status of a bootblack must personally accept responsibility. Each is considered ultimately free to shape his own destiny, and each is held personally accountable for the use of his freedom.

Chapter three will discuss the sources of the individualistic morality and free-will image of man in some detail. For the present, we may note that Christian religiosity and political conservatism appear to be its prime sources. Max Weber first examined the religious roots of this image in his study of the "spirit of capitalism," tracing the evolution of a predestinarian Calvinism into a religious ethic of hard work and the demonstration of inner worth.[1] The role of political conservatism may be seen in its valuation of "rugged individualism" and its opposition to any social legislation which would limit the unfettered exercise of individual freedom. The conservative's

1. Max Weber, *The Protestant Ethic and the Spirit of Capitalism*, trans. Talcott Parsons (New York: Charles Scribner's Sons, 1958).

discussion of "morality" (or its decline) almost always reflects a belief in man's ultimate freedom and personal responsibility for his actions.

This individualistic morality, then, is based on a special theory of human behavior. The source of a man's actions is to be found in his total being: his personal character, his inner strength, his courage, and so forth. The unit of analysis in such a theory is the total human individual.

The Scientific Challenge and the New Social Morality

Many primitive world-views regard virtually all objects in terms of a theory of behavior similar to that outlined above. Animals, trees, plants, and inanimate objects are believed to act in terms of their individual wills and motivations. When lightning strikes a tree, the answer is sought in terms of the lightning's motivations: Why did it desire to destroy the tree? Similar explanations are offered to explain why the sun chooses to rise every morning, move across the sky, and finally set in the west at day's end. Each object is viewed as having an independent will, and all events in the environment are explained in terms of those wills.

Western science, of course, operates from a totally different perspective. A deterministic rather than a free-will posture is assumed. All events have causes which determine them. Moreover, the links between causes and effects follow determinable natural laws. If lightning strikes a tree, this is caused by the disposition of electrical charges in the area and by the laws of electricity. Neither the lightning nor the tree is given a personality or an independent will.

When science seeks to explain events and the relations between objects, the events and objects are often broken down into components or aspects quite foreign to common sense. In the present example, the tree is not a tree in any total sense; it is only an elevated source of electrical charges. The tree in its totality, then, is not the unit of analysis; only certain of its attributes—its elevation and its electrical charge—are the units of analysis.

Today, the application of the scientific perspective to physical events and objects would seem to pose little threat to human morality, although this was not always the case. The present threat to morality exists in the application of the scientific perspective to human behavior. When a deterministic model of human behavior is advanced, the old individualistic morality is struck at its very base.

Modern social science disavows the individualistic theory of behavior and the individual person as the unit of analysis. Herbert McClosky has discussed the social scientific orientation with reference to political science, and his discussion is relevant to other social sciences as well.

It is impossible to understand any man, much less any group of men, all at once and in his (or their) entirety. Since every man is potentially many things, plays many roles, behaves differently in different contexts, and holds various and often conflicting beliefs, he cannot possibly be understood as a "totality." His behavior cannot be explained by describing everything about him at once, even if it were physically possible to do so. When one asks what "causes" a political actor to behave in a certain way, one expects an answer in terms of some specific force that one has reason to believe is relevant to that particular type of behavior.[2]

From this perspective, then, the total human being is not the unit of analysis any more than the total tree was the unit of analysis in the previous example. Nor is the ultimate source of human behavior to be found in the idiosyncratic character of the individual actor any more than the tree's idiosyncratic character was relevant to its being struck by lightning. Generalized social attributes, rather than individual human beings,

2. Herbert McClosky, "Survey Research in Political Science," *Survey Research in the Social Sciences,* ed. Charles Y. Glock (New York: Russell Sage Foundation, 1967), p. 136.

are the units of analysis. Typical attributes for social scientific analysis are age, sex, occupation, religion, education, region of upbringing, and so forth.

The social scientist, then, views social attributes as the determinants of human behavior. Thus, a man's voting behavior is determined by such attributes as his occupation, education, and the region in which he was raised. The key to his behavior is *not* sought in his inner character or his total being.

When we consider that many of the variables frequently singled out in this regard are those over which the actor has little or no control, the threat to the traditional, individualistic morality is clear. If certain actions are largely determined by, say, a person's sex, age, and birthplace, how can that person be held personally accountable for those actions? If the individual's free will is discounted, so must his responsibility be discounted. If the deterministic image of man, fostered by social science, is substantially correct, then the old morality is inappropriate and must be replaced by a new social morality commensurate with the deterministic theory of behavior.

Charles Y. Glock has been especially sensitive to the increased acceptance of the deterministic image of man and the new social morality accompanying it. He writes:

> The changes wrought so far by this emerging image of man have been greatest in those parts of our society which are most subject to being informed by social scientists. Particularly affected have been those institutions whose task it is to deal with the problems of so-called "deviant behavior" in society. Ideas about ways to deal with the delinquent, the poverty stricken, the mentally ill, the criminal have changed radically over the last generation. No longer, for example, is charity animated by a concept that the poor are poor through some fault of their own, through a failure to meet their responsibilities as free men. In fact, we no longer feel comfortable with the word "charity." [3]

3. Charles Y. Glock, "Images of Man and Public Opinion," *Public Opinion Quarterly,* Winter 1964, p. 545.

One might add that in precisely those areas where the new social morality—based on a deterministic image of man—has had its greatest impact to date, one also finds the strongest reaffirmations of the traditional, individualistic morality. In recent years, the U.S. Supreme Court has been frequently and angrily criticized for "coddling criminals." Responsibility for poverty, and especially the poverty of the Blacks, is still laid at the door of the impoverished. "Most people, in trying to find the causes of the summer's race riots and the problems of the Negroes have blamed the white population. They claim we have deprived Negroes and have discriminated, taking all the good jobs and the good houses leaving them with the rats. . . . Now Negroes are demanding that the white population build them new houses, give them jobs and kill the rats. Why can't they kill their own rats?" [4]

Organization of Part Two

Despite the often bitter reactions against the deterministic image of man and the growth of the new social morality, the trend would seem ultimately irresistible. The links between science and determinism are so strong that if science continues to prosper in America, social determinism will similarly prosper. This prospect raises two important questions for medicine.

First, what is the relation between medical science and the new social morality? The behavioral sciences are of necessity based on a deterministic image of man—but is medical science? Although medical scientists must view the materials of their researches from a deterministic perspective, it is conceivable that they might limit their acceptance of determinism to cells, tissues, and organs, holding man to be governed by different rules.

Second, what are the effects of the new social morality for medical relations in America? There is no denying that the

4. A letter to the *San Francisco Chronicle*, September 6, 1967.

traditional, individualistic morality has been important to medical relations in the past. Patients and physicians have interacted with one another as total human beings, each being held personally accountable for his actions. How will the new social morality change this? Part two is devoted to answering these two questions.

Chapter three examines the extent to which scientific orientations among medical school faculty members are related to the rise of a new social morality in America. We begin by noting the incompatibility of science and traditional religious and political perspectives. Then we shall turn to a consideration of the new social morality as such. The determinism implicit in medical science will be seen to relate strongly to the more deterministic social morality. We may conclude, therefore, that the rise of science in medicine also signals the growing prominence of the new morality among physicians.

Chapter four considers the implications of the new morality for humane patient care. What will it do to the physician's compassion, responsibility, and respect for experimental subjects? On the one hand, one might expect that the denigration of the individual which lies at the base of the new social morality would lead faculty members to be less compassionate (viewing patients in terms of variables rather than as sacred, total human beings), less responsible (lacking respect for the patient and not feeling personally accountable for their own professional behavior) and less sensitive to the norm of experimenter participation in dangerous experiments (again, lacking respect for the subject as a sacred human being).

On the other hand, one might expect the new social morality to have just the opposite effect. Many would argue that the new social morality is more humane in that it relieves individuals of the blame for situations they themselves could not control. Conceivably the individualistic morality may lead some physicians to blame patients for being ill; the new social morality would make physicians more sympathetic. Chapter four will test these two possibilities by examining the effects of both scientific orientations and social morality on responses to the items which were examined in chapter two.

Having examined the implications of the new social morality for humane patient care in a face-to-face context, part three will be devoted to an appraisal of the broader, long-range implications.

CHAPTER THREE

The Bases of Scientific Medicine

The primary concern of part one was to test some rather specific allegations regarding a conflict between science and morality in medicine. The analyses, however, did not confirm the expected conflict. Despite the findings of chapter two, there are, nevertheless, good reasons to suspect that science and morality conflict. Certainly the history of science presents countless examples of scientists clashing with the traditional morality of their time and often being censured for it. We need only list the names of Socrates, Galileo, Copernicus, Darwin, and Freud to demonstrate the previous conflict. Is one to assume, then, that such conflict has ceased altogether in our time?

This chapter advances the thesis that the conflict between science and traditional morality continues and may be observed among the sample of medical school faculty members. The conflict, however, is not so much one of morality per se as a reflection of the different ontological beliefs supported by traditional morality, on the one hand, and science, on the other. The traditional value-systems of American society are based on beliefs about the nature of man which directly oppose the basic beliefs upon which rational-empirical science is founded. Thus, we shall note, that teaching physicians who are uncommitted to the traditional value-systems are the most likely to be committed to science. The traditional value-systems and science are largely incompatible.

The reason for the observed incompatibility lies primarily in the realm of beliefs about man's freedom. The traditional value-systems are based on the belief that man, as an individual, is free to control his own destiny; he is the master of his fate. The logic of rational-empirical science, however, requires a deterministic perspective which limits the individual freedom posited by traditional values. The scientist believes that man's actions are largely the product of his environment and his past. Such a view directly conflicts with the free-will image of man, which has predominated in the past.

Religion and politics have been the primary carriers of the traditional beliefs about man in America. Thus, we should expect that commitment to traditional religious and political perspectives would decrease scientific orientations among teaching physicians. Our analysis will begin at this point. Having examined the relationships between religion, politics, and science, we shall then consider more directly the images of man which those several perspectives represent.

Religion and Science

Religion and science have clashed throughout history.[1] The Socratic drama of ancient Greece represented an early collision of religious faith and rational inquiry. Later men of

1. For an excellent historical account, see A. D. White, *A History of the Warfare of Science and Theology in Christendom* (New York: Dover, 1960). Bernhard J. Stern provides an account of similar warfare in medical science in *Social Factors in Medical Progress* (New York: Columbia University Press), 1927.

science such as Galileo, Copernicus, and Darwin faced severe charges of religious heresy. And in the twentieth century, the Scopes "monkey trial" in Dayton, Tennessee, attests the continuing conflict between scientific and religious perspectives.

For the most part, these conflicts have been seen as disputes over specific conclusions about reality. Does the earth revolve around the sun or vice versa? Is man descended from lower animals? Religious tradition and scientific inquiry have produced disparate conclusions, and the two sides have vied for credibility.

This chapter suggests that an important contemporary conflict between religion and science concerns the extent of man's freedom. Science is based on a deterministic view of man, as discussed earlier. From the scientific perspective, man's actions may be attributed to social forces and other environmental factors, which he cannot control and often does not experience consciously. The religious perspective, however, cannot wholly incorporate the deterministic image of man. Charles Y. Glock and Rodney Stark concede that all religions acknowledge a degree of control on the part of their gods, but the authors note that "In all religions, man is left with considerable control of his own destiny." [2] Often this belief is essential to religious moral codes and as a justification for religious rewards and punishments.

The belief that man is possessed of extensive free will shifts the burden of responsibility and accountability to man. It makes meaningful both the establishment of standards of right and wrong and the universal religious injunction against sin. Together with the belief in God's ultimacy, it also gives meaning to religion's systems of eternal rewards and punishments and to the commitment which these systems generate. Only within a free-will image of man can man be held accountable for his actions, and only if man is ac-

2. Charles Y. Glock and Rodney Stark, *Religion and Society in Tension* (Chicago: Rand McNally & Co., 1965), p. 296.

countable can religion command his allegiance and commitment.[3]

To the extent that free will is postulated as a justification for otherworldly rewards and punishments, this religious motif would not likely conflict with either natural or social science. Yet, as described in the Weberian thesis regarding the Protestant ethic, men have been impatient with the waiting to determine whether their free will was used well or badly.[4] In the search for more immediate indications of salvation, the free-will doctrine was extended down from Heaven and up from Hell. Out of the originally predestinarian Calvinism came the doctrine that a man's worldly successes and failures were evidence of his distant reward. Worldly success became the measure of a man's inner worth.

At the base of this perspective, then, was the belief that a man's behavior was largely subject to his own control. The early settlers in the new world clearly accepted this belief, and their actions seemed to substantiate its validity. The rugged men of the frontier seemed living proof of man's free will. So did the rags-to-riches business tycoons.

Social science now largely denies the validity of this belief. Social scientific research increasingly points to social structural explanations for human behavior. The very concepts "role," "norm," and "socialization" deny the soul-searching idiosyncrasy of each human action. From the social scientific perspective, man acts primarily in accord with the ways he was taught to act and in accord with the constraints placed on him by his environment. The element of social determinism implied by this perpective, of course, contradicts the holistic assignment of freedom and accountability to each individual.

The clash of perspectives is clearest with regard to religion and *social* science. Yet one might expect that all science, since

3. *Ibid.,* p. 297.
4. Max Weber, *The Protestant Ethic and the Spirit of Capitalism,* trans. Talcott Parsons (New York: Charles Scribner's Sons, 1958).

all sciences are deterministic, might be incompatible with religious perspectives. A large body of research findings, moreover, suggest that this is indeed the case.[5] In one of the more recent examinations of this issue, Glock and Stark found that university graduate students declined in their religious commitments over the course of academic studies. Consistently, they found that those students most exposed to scientific scholarship were the least religious.[6]

Medical science, like other sciences, is based on a deterministic perspective. The medical researcher believes that good and poor health are determined by factors that are beyond the patient's control and which can be isolated by scientific examination. We might conclude, therefore, that religious faculty members in the present study would be unlikely to exhibit scientific orientations. At the same time, we should entertain the possibility that many are able to compartmentalize their professional and religious perspectives. Quite conceivably, a faculty member might accept the determinism involved in disease, all the while believing that human behavior does not follow the same deterministic rules.

To permit an examination of the relationship between religious and scientific perspectives, faculty members were asked to evaluate their own religious commitments. "In general, how important would you say your religion is to you?" They were asked to select one of four possible answers: extremely important, fairly important, fairly unimportant, or not at all important.

Table 15 suggests that scientific and religious perspectives are somewhat incompatible even in medicine. Among those who said their religion was "extremely important," 45 percent were scored high (2 or 3) on the index of scientific orienta-

5. For a short but excellent review of the research literature, see Glock and Stark, *Religion and Society in Tension,* pp. 265–266.
6. *Ibid.,* pp. 262–288.

tions. This percentage increases across the table, with 70 percent scored scientific among those whose religion is "not at all important."

TABLE 15

RELIGIOSITY AND SCIENTIFIC ORIENTATIONS

	Question: How important is your religion to you?			
	Extremely important	Fairly important	Fairly un-important	Not at all important
Percentage scientists*	45 (75)	57 (136)	70 (125)	70 (87)

Note: Number in parentheses represents number of cases on which percentage is based.
* Percentage scored 2 or 3 on the index of scientific orientations.

These data confirm the general expectation that religious faculty members would be less oriented to science than those for whom religion is not important. On one level, this may be interpreted as another conflict between faith and rational inquiry. The thesis advanced in this book suggests that it is more than that: that the different images of man prescribed by religion and science provide the explanation for the observed incompatibility.

One way of testing this thesis is to examine the relationship between science and faculty members' religious affiliations. While all religions posit a degree of freedom to man, this doctrine is more important to some religions than to others. It was suggested earlier that the free-will image of man prevalent in American society grew out of the Protestant ethic examined by Weber. Therefore, one would expect to find Protestant faculty members less able to accept a scientific perspective.

This expectation is subject to modification, however, in the light of other research findings. First, Robert K. Merton has suggested that Protestantism, historically at least, provided support for scientific inquiry while Catholicism did not. In his examination of religious affiliations and scientific achievement in seventeenth century England and elsewhere, he found an affinity between the values of Protestantism and science.

> In every instance, the association of Protestantism with scientific and technologic interests and achievements is pronounced, even when extra-religious influences are as far as possible eliminated. The association is largely understandable in terms of the norms embodied in both systems. The positive estimation of Protestants of a hardly disguised utilitarianism, of intra-mundane interests, of a thoroughgoing empiricism, of the right and even the duty of *libre examen,* and of the explicit individual questioning of authority were congenial to the same values found in modern science.[7]

Merton's analysis, of course, did not consider the effects of the free-will and deterministic images of man as such. And his conclusions were drawn from data representing an earlier era than the one which now concerns us. Nevertheless, more recent research substantiates his findings regarding the scientific orientations of Protestants and Catholics. The study by Glock and Stark noted earlier found Roman Catholic graduate students the least likely to respond to the scientific scholarship of graduate school.

Glock and Stark went beyond Protestants and Catholics, however, to examine Jews and agnostics. The latter two groups were found to be more scientific than either Protestants or Catholics. Other research, moreover, substantiates their findings.[8]

7. Robert K. Merton, *Social Theory and Social Structure* (New York: Free Press, 1957), p. 595.
8. Bernard Barber has discussed the scientific orientations of Jews in *Science and the Social Order* (Glencoe, Ill.: Free Press, 1952), pp. 136–137. See also Lois-Ellin Datta, "Family Religious Background and Early Scientific Creativity," *American Sociological Review,* August 1967, pp. 626–635. Less attention has been paid to agnostics in the sociological study of religion.

The consistent finding that Catholics are low on scientific orientations has normally been attributed to a greater resistance to the rational inquiry inherent in science. This was Merton's thesis, and others have suggested similar explanations. Other evidence suggests that the image-of-man thesis advanced here may explain the observed relationships.

In a study of attitudes toward de facto school segregation in a Western community, Rankin, Babbie, and Glock sought an explanation in terms of free-will and deterministic images of man.[9] Those who were opposed to government attempts to eradicate de facto segregation in the local school system frequently defended their position, saying that Negroes were responsible for "making it on their own." As the researchers expected, Protestant members of the community were very likely to express this belief in man's control over his own destiny. So were the Roman Catholics in the sample. The researchers tentatively concluded that the free-will image of man was widely accepted by middle-class Catholics as well as by Protestants. Jews and agnostics in the study were the least likely to support the free-will image. Rather, they suggested that Negroes were the victims of the social system, and that the system itself ought to be changed.

Returning to the sample of teaching physicians, then, we might expect Protestants and Roman Catholic faculty members to score relatively low on scientific orientations, while the Jews and agnostics should be more scientific. Such a finding would support the thesis that scientific orientations are largely dependent on an acceptance of determinism in human affairs. Table 16 provides confirmation of the thesis.

Catholic faculty members are the least science-oriented of

9. Robert P. Rankin, Earl R. Babbie, and Charles Y. Glock, "Images of Man and de facto Segregation," Berkeley: Survey Research Center monograph M-14, presented to the Society for the Study of Social Problems, in Montreal, August 29, 1964.

TABLE 16

RELIGIOUS AFFILIATION AND SCIENTIFIC ORIENTATIONS

	Religious affiliation			
	Catholic	Protestant	Jew	None
Percentage scientists	54	58	77	61
	(74)	(203)	(81)	(62)

Note: Number in parentheses represents number of cases on which percentage is based.

all the four groups. This finding coincides with the results of previous research in this area. Protestants are slightly more oriented to science, although they differ from the Catholics by only four percentage points. The Jewish faculty are clearly the most scientific with over three-fourths scoring either *2* or *3* on the index.

The agnostic faculty—those reporting no religious affiliation—fall between the Protestants and Jews in scientific orientations—nearer the former than the latter. They are, of course, the most difficult group to discuss. While each of the other religious groups has a tradition which can be described and analyzed, such an approach is not possible with regard to the agnostics. It does not make sense to discuss the intellectual traditions of agnosticism, although one might be tempted to do so. Given the religious profile of the United States past and present, it seems more than likely that the agnostics in this sample come from families which professed one of the three major faiths. While these faculty members may represent the beginnings of a new religious tradition,[10] it still does not make

10. In the Glock-Stark study reported earlier, "none" was the second largest religious group among the sample of graduate students. Only the Protestants (38 percent) were more prominent than the agnostics (26 percent). It may indeed make sense to speak of a new major faith in America, at least among its most educated members. (See Glock and Stark, *Religion and Society in Tension*, p. 269.)

sense to view them as the product of an agnostic tradition. Most undoubtedly were raised in Protestant, Catholic, or Jewish homes.

The ambiguous character of the agnostic faculty members' religious histories may explain the fact that they are not the most scientific group of all. This is what we should have expected if they represented an agnostic tradition. As it is, we may only say that their current religious status does not prevent them from assuming the deterministic posture required by science, although the religious training of some may still have that effect.

The clearest finding in these latest data is the relatively non-scientific orientation of Catholics and Protestants. These are the two groups which were believed to be most committed to the free-will image of man and hence the most resistant to the determinism of science. The findings of tables 15 and 16, then, tentatively support the thesis that medical science is incompatible with the traditional religious image of man as a free-will agent.

One alternative possibility remains to be checked. We recall that Merton claimed that Protestantism, compared with Catholicism, provided a positive support for science. The most recent data confirm Merton's ranking of these two groups in scientific orientations. If, however, he is correct in saying that Protestant values provide a positive support for science, this would go against the thesis proposed by this book. In terms of the image-of-man thesis, Protestant values—support for the free-will image of man—should hinder rather than support scientific orientations.

It will be recalled from table 15 that religious commitment overall has a negative effect on scientific orientations. Merton's thesis, however, is that *among Protestants* religious involvement and scientific orientations should be positively associated. In his discussion of Puritanism and science, Merton suggests that "the mere fact that an individual is *nominally* a Catholic or a Protestant has no bearing upon his attitudes toward science. . . . It is the firm acceptance of the values basic to the two creeds which accounts for the difference in the respective scientific contributions of Catholics and Protestants." [11] While the present study provides no sure measure of "the firm acceptance of the values basic to the two creeds," faculty members' self-evaluation of their religiosity should provide an approximate test of the Mertonian thesis. Protestant faculty who say their religion is extremely important to them should be more scientific than those who say it is not at all important. Among Catholics, the relationship should be reversed.

TABLE 17

RELIGIOUS AFFILIATION, RELIGIOSITY, AND
SCIENTIFIC ORIENTATIONS

Religious Affiliation	Percentage Scientists			
	Question: How important is your religion to you?			
	Extremely important	Fairly important	Fairly un-important	Not at all important
Catholic	44	60	62	*
	(32)	(25)	(13)	(4)
Protestant	47	54	65	71
	(36)	(80)	(69)	(17)
Jew	*	68	88	93
	(6)	(28)	(32)	(14)

Note: Number in parentheses represents number of cases on which percentage is based.
* Too few cases in these cells for stable percentages.

Table 17 contradicts Merton's thesis regarding Protestantism and science. Among Protestant faculty, as among the

11. Merton, *Social Theory*, pp. 587–588.

other two groups, scientific orientations decrease with increasing religiosity. Less than half of the most religious Protestants are scored as scientific, compared with nearly three-fourths of the least religious. Although these data in no way challenge Merton's conclusions regarding the rise of science in seventeenth century England, they do indicate that a different situation pertains today.

None of the three major religious faiths, then, can be said to positively support scientific orientations among medical school faculty members. The more religious a man is in any religion, the less likely he is to be scientific. Yet, at the same time, we have seen that Catholicism, Protestantism, and Judaism retard science differentially. Judaism would appear to be the least detrimental, and Catholicism the most. In a sense, then, these findings confirm the expectations derived from previous research, but the "contribution" of one religious perspective over another must be viewed somewhat more critically.

The preceding examination of religion and science among medical school faculty members supports the thesis that scientific orientations are based on a more deterministic image of man than is typical of religious perspectives. Religions, and particularly Christianity, posit the view that man is the master of his own destiny and hence responsible for his own behavior. This view is incompatible with deterministic science.

We shall return in a moment to examine the moral implications of these findings. First, the analysis will turn briefly to another American value-system which is related to the traditional image of man: politics.

Politics and Science

The possibility of a relationship between politics and science has not received the social science attention accorded religion and science. Indeed, there would seem to be no research precedents for the present examination. Nevertheless, the image-of-man thesis being advanced in this book suggests that a relationship ought to exist.

If scientific orientations are incompatible with the free-will image of man, then faculty members holding conservative political beliefs ought not to be scientific. More explicitly than any religious orientation, conservative American politics have stressed the freedom and responsibility of the individual. Particularly in its rightmost wing, the Republican party has differed most from the Democratic party in its opposition to social legislation based on a deterministic view of man. (Conservative Democrats have, of course, joined them in that opposition.) On issues of Negro civil rights, poverty, education, medical care, housing, and so forth, the American conservative position has been that everyone must take care of himself, as he is believed to be inherently capable of doing.

Teaching physicians in the present study were asked to assess their own political orientations along a conservative–liberal continuum. They were asked, "How do you tend to think of yourself politically?" and were provided with four categories: very conservative, moderately conservative, moderately liberal, and very liberal. It is a fair assessment to say that most teaching physicians are "moderates" politically. Nearly nine out of ten replied they were either moderately conservative or moderately liberal, although the majority of all faculty said moderately liberal (54 percent).

Table 18 confirms the expectation that conservative political views are incompatible with scientific orientations. Although only eight faculty described themselves as "very conservative," they have been presented separately in the table for descriptive interest. Only three out of the eight (38 percent) were scored as scientific. Scientific orientations increase steadily as we move across the table in the direction of liberal political perspectives. Seventy-three percent of the "very liberal" teaching physicians were scored as scientific.

TABLE 18

POLITICS AND SCIENTIFIC ORIENTATIONS

| | Question: How do you tend to think of yourself politically? | | | |
	Very con- servative	Moderately con- servative	Moderately liberal	Very liberal
Percentage scientists	38 (8)*	52 (142)	67 (227)	73 (45)

Note: Number in parentheses represents number of cases on which percentage is based.

* Note the small number of cases in this cell. Percentage is presented here for descriptive interest only.

These data on political perspectives further confirm the thesis that scientific orientations depend on a deterministic image of man. Those faculty members who are committed to either religious or political perspectives which posit a free-will image of man are thereby limited in their ability to be scientists.

Images of Man and Social Morality

If the religious and political perspectives discussed above were only ontological belief systems, then the findings of this analysis might be judged relevant only to matters of scientific recruitment. Indeed, they have a far greater significance for American society and, by extension, for medicine. The free-will image of man supported by Christian religiosity and conservative politics provides the foundation for the traditional individualistic American morality discussed earlier, and the individualistic morality of America's past is being replaced by another morality from that same history.

Seymour M. Lipset has concluded that the two basic values of *achievement* and *equality* have been of the utmost importance in American society throughout its history.[12] The former is reflected in such terms as "rugged individualism" and "self-made man" and in the pragmatism frequently attributed to Americans. The notion of achievement is reasonably simple to understand; equality, however, tends to be more ambiguous. Especially in political terms, political philosophers have struggled over the meaning of equality in American life. It has been suggested variously that the term refers to "equality of rewards," "equality of opportunity," or simply an equal right to vote. Some have suggested an even more restricted interpretation.

Whatever the interpretation given to the notion of equality in our society, it should be clear that the two values are somewhat incompatible. At its base, the value of achievement represents the freedom to acquire inequality, to get more or to go farther than other people. If equality is taken to mean "equality of rewards," then the notion of achievement is denied altogether. If only "equality of opportunity" is intended, achievement becomes a "one-generation" concept, with parents unable to pass on special advantages to their children. Even the equality of voting conflicted with the early American practice of reserving the franchise for property owners. Thus, the values of achievement and equality have conflicted throughout our national history, yet each has persisted.

In practice, the value of equality has coincided with a socially deterministic image of man. First, in the context of the Negro civil rights movement and then in the "war against poverty," we have witnessed a national debate regarding the degree of personal accountability that can be assigned to the individual. Proponents of the civil rights movement and of antipoverty measures have argued that Negroes and the poor

12. Seymour M. Lipset, *The First New Nation* (New York: Basic Books, 1963); see p. 102, for example.

have been the victims of social circumstances quite beyond their control.

Voices on the other side of the debate have opposed all forms of social welfare or "social engineering." If people are poor, it is argued, it is because they are lazy. The answer to poverty is hard work. (Ironically, the stereotyped belief that "all Negroes are lazy" is used to support the position of individual responsibility rather than the deterministic position.)

The new social morality, based on a belief in social determinism and a desire for equality, ought to be related to scientific perspectives. It was stated earlier that the *social* sciences have importantly fostered the deterministic view, but the data regarding religion, politics, and science suggests that the rise of *medical* science may also be associated with the new social morality, at least indirectly.

Although social scientists have assumed a deterministic posture in their own research for years, it is only recently that they have begun studying images of man per se. As a result, we have yet to discover adequate means for identifying the free-will and deterministic images among the public. Nevertheless, two questions asked in the present survey of faculty members provide a rough indication of the two views.

First, faculty members were asked to agree or disagree with the following statement: "Willpower is the essential force for overcoming social difficulties." This statement was intended to reflect the traditional free-will notion that man's successes or failures depend on his inner worth, his willpower. Agreement with this statement, then, should indicate an acceptance of the free-will image of man. Disagreement, on the other hand, reflects at least some deterministic reservations.

The second item dealing with the two images of man focused on a more specific issue. While Negroes have been accused of a lack of initiative and willpower, the same charge has been lodged against welfare recipients. Some of the more radical opponents of welfare have suggested from time to time that if all payments were stopped, the unemployed would very quickly find jobs. It is charged that welfare recipients are getting a free ride from society, living off the fat of the land, as it were. This line of reasoning is also clearly based on the belief that man's lot is not determined by his environment, but only reflects his own innate abilities and personal drive. As such, it is informed by what we have called the free-will image of man. To tap this orientation, teaching physicians were asked to agree or disagree with another statement: "Most people on welfare could take care of themselves if they really wanted to."

Taken at face value, each of these statements provides an indication of faculty members' images of man: either as a free-will agent or as a product of his environment. Each item is, of course, subject to reservations. Neither should be taken as an indication of extreme commitments to either free will or determinism. Nevertheless, they should indicate faculty members' general inclinations in one direction or the other.

One thing can be said for certain: responses to the two items

TABLE 19

MEASURING IMAGES OF MAN

	"Most people on welfare could take care of themselves"			
	Strongly agree	Agree	Disagree	Strongly disagree
Percentage who agree that "willpower is the essential force for overcoming social difficulties"	92 (12)	66 (74)	24 (202)	10 (126)

Note: Number in parentheses represents number of cases on which percentage is based.

are highly related to one another. As table 19 shows, among those who strongly agree that welfare recipients are capable of caring for themselves, 92 percent agree that willpower is the essential force for overcoming difficulties. Of those who strongly disagree with the first statement, only one in ten agrees with the second.

To permit a further examination of the implications of teaching physicians' images of man, an index was created from responses to the two items.[13] Each faculty member, therefore, has been scored as leaning toward one or the other view, or as holding an intermediate position.

Our earlier analyses of religion and science hypothesized that certain religious orientations reflected a commitment to the traditional image of man as a free-will agent. The creation of an image-of-man index now offers an opportunity for testing that hypothesis. Table 20 presents the relationships between religious affiliation and religiosity, on the one hand, and images of man on the other.

The first half of table 20 shows that the two least scientific religious groups—the Protestants and the Catholics—are the least deterministic as well. Only 18 percent of the Catholics and 30 percent of the Protestants are scored as "deterministic" in their responses to the image-of-man items. On the other hand, they are the most likely groups to exhibit an acceptance of the traditional free-will image of man.

The second half of the table confirms the hypothesis regarding religiosity and determinism. Acceptance of a deterministic image of man decreases with increasing religiosity. Religious

13. Responses to both questions were scored as follows: strongly agree, 3; agree, 2; disagree, 1; strongly disagree, 0. In view of the distribution of scores on the index, it was necessary to collapse the scores into three categories: Deterministic (01), Intermediate (23), and Free Will (456). This method was chosen instead of collapsing response categories prior to indexing because a careful examination of the bivariate relationship between the two items indicated that *degree* of agreement or disagreement ought to be taken into account.

TABLE 20

RELIGION AND IMAGES OF MAN

Image-of-Man Index	Religious Affiliation			
	Catholic	Protestant	Jew	None
Deterministic: *0–1*	18%	30%	53%	40%
Intermediate: *2–3*	59	52	42	47
Free will: *4–6*	23	18	5	13
100% =	(71)	(194)	(79)	(62)

Image-of-Man Index	"How important is your religion to you?"			
	Extremely important	Fairly important	Fairly un-important	Not at all important
Deterministic: *0–1*	25%	29%	38%	45%
Intermediate: *2–3*	58	54	47	43
Free will: *4–6*	17	17	15	12
100% =	(71)	(134)	(118)	(89)

Note: Number in parentheses represents number of cases on which percentage is based.

faculty members are the most likely to hold the free-will image.

Table 21 confirms the hypothesis regarding politics and images of man. None of the very conservative faculty members were scored "deterministic" on the index, compared with 62 percent of the very liberal. The belief that man is the master of his destiny is a tenet of American political conservatism.

In view of the demonstrated relationships between religion and politics and faculty images of man, an index was created to test the cumulative effect of both religion and politics. Faculty were given one point on the index (*a*) for identifying themselves as either Catholic or Protestant, and (*b*) for saying their religion was at least "fairly important." In addition, faculty received two points for characterizing themselves as either "very conservative" or "moderately conservative."

TABLE 21

POLITICS AND IMAGES OF MAN

Image-of-Man Index	Political Orientations			
	Very con-servative	Moderately con-servative	Moderately liberal	Very liberal
Deterministic: *0–1*	0%	17%	41%	62%
Intermediate: *2–3*	57	55	50	36
Free will: *4–6*	43	28	9	2
100% =	(7)*	(134)	(222)	(44)

Note: Number in parentheses represents number of cases on which percentage is based.
* Note the small number of cases upon which the percentages in this column are based. They have been presented here for descriptive interest only.

(These responses were combined because of the small number of "very conservative" faculty members.) Since table 18 indicated a significant difference in the orientations of "moderately liberal" and "very liberal" faculty members, the former were given one point, while the latter received none.

The result of this scoring procedure was a composite index of religious and political orientations to the free-will image of man. Those scored *4* were considered the most oriented to that image. Table 22 shows that religion and politics are cumulatively related to the images of man.

Among those least oriented to the free-will image of man (scored *0*), two-thirds are deterministic in terms of the two attitudinal items. This percentage decreases steadily across the table to only 13 percent among those most oriented (scored *4*) to the free-will image.

The substantive importance of these findings should not be lost in the examination of the statistical association between two indexes. It is the contention of this book that a new social morality is becoming predominant in American society. It is

TABLE 22

RELIGION, POLITICS, AND IMAGES OF MAN

Image-of-Man Index:	Index of Religious and Political Orientations to the Free-Will Image				
	Low 0	1	2	3	High 4
Deterministic: *0–1*	66%	49%	39%	27%	13%
Intermediate: *2–3*	34	45	48	52	61
Free will: *4–6*	0	6	13	21	26
100% =	(29)	(69)	(95)	(131)	(75)

Note: Number in parentheses represents number of cases on which percentage is based.

increasingly displacing the traditional, individualistic morality of our national past. The two items indicating faculty members' images of man might also be regarded as indicators of the two moralities.

The faculty member who supports the concept of social welfare indicates at least a partial commitment to the new social morality. The faculty member who believes welfare recipients could take care of themselves if they really wanted to represents the individualistic morality of the past. A similar case could be made with regard to faculty members' beliefs about the importance of willpower.

Although woefully inadequate, the image-of-man index provides at least a tentative measure of the individualistic and deterministic moralities currently conflicting in American society. Since the past half-century or so in America has been marked by a general liberalization of both religion and politics, it is only reasonable to conclude that support for the new morality—based on a more deterministic image of man—is on the increase. Indeed, the growth of social welfare legislation and the increasingly deterministic view of deviance gives more direct proof that the trend is toward the new social morality and away from the individualistic morality of earlier years.

How does all this relate to medicine? It was suggested earlier that the rise of science in medicine coincides with the ascendancy of the new social morality in America. Indeed, we have seen that the religious and political perspectives associated with the old, individualistic moralty are incompatible with science. Science depends, instead, on the deterministic perspective which lies at the base of the new social morality.

TABLE 23

SCIENTIFIC ORIENTATIONS—BY IMAGES OF MAN
AND ORIENTATIONS TO FREE WILL

Religious and Political Orientations to the Free-Will Image	Percentage Scientists		
	Image-of-Man Index		
	Deter-ministic	Inter-mediate	Free will
Low *0*	83 (18)	80 (10)	*
1	78 (32)	73 (30)	† (4)
2	66 (35)	71 (45)	50 (12)
3	63 (32)	55 (62)	46 (26)
High *4*	50 (10)	50 (46)	44 (18)

Note: Number in parentheses represents number of cases on which percentage is based.
* There are no cases in this cell.
† Too few cases in this cell for a stable percentage.

Table 23 shows that both the image-of-man index and the composite index of religious and political orientations to the free-will image are related to scientific orientations among our sample of teaching physicians. Among those least disposed to the free-will image and designated as deterministic on the image-of-man index, 83 percent were scored as scientific. At the other extreme of the table—highly oriented to the free-will image and designated as holding it—only 44 percent are scientific.

In terms of the thesis advanced in this chapter, we should expect that religious and political orientations would have no effect on science save that of the images of man they reflect. Table 23 does not support this. Regardless of faculty members' images of man, as measured by the two attitude questions, the original relationships between religious and political perspectives and scientific orientations are maintained. In part, this no doubt reflects the inadequacy of the image-of-man index. A better index, constructed from more valid items, might have better interpreted the religious and political effects. At the same time, it would seem likely that religion and politics conflict with science for other reasons, and even a perfect measure of images of man would not erase that conflict.

For present purposes, the most important fact lies in the overall relationship between scientific orientations and the several bases of the old and new moralities. The rise of scientific medicine coincides with the decline of the traditional, individualistic morality and its replacement by a new, more deterministic morality. Scientific faculty members are the least likely to uphold the traditional morality, their primary commitment being to the new one.

The overall shift in social morality examined in this chapter would seem to have important implications for issues of medical morality such as the traditional norms of humane patient care. Does the demise of the traditional morality forewarn of a future demise of compassion, responsibility, and respect for human worth? The examination of science and patient care in chapter two showed that science per se does not threaten the traditional norms. But does the new morality?

Chapter four will examine the joint effects of science and the new social morality on the norms of humane patient care. To facilitate that analysis, it will be useful to create a new composite index, which may be taken to represent the two social moralities, old and new. While the bases of the two moral systems lie in faculty members' images of man as free or largely determined, the influence of religious and political factors ought to be taken into account as well. Indeed, the decline of the traditional, individualistic morality coincides with the decline of traditional religious and political value-systems. For purposes of the present analysis, then, we combine the image-of-man index (created from the two attitude items) and the index of religious and political orientations to the free-will image. This has been accomplished by adding to the religious and political orientations index scores: 2 points for holding the free-will image on the attitude index, 1 point for holding the intermediate image, and 0 points for the deterministic image.

The resultant free-will image-of-man index has a range of scores from 0 to 6. The higher scores on the new index represent a commitment to the traditional image of man as a free-will agent and to the traditional, individualistic morality. The lower scores on the index represent a commitment to the deterministic image of man and to the new social morality based upon it.

The reader must recognize that this new composite index is little more than an approximation of the variables it is intended to represent. Hopefully, future examinations of this topic will be availed of more direct indicators of the old and new moralities and the ontological beliefs which lie at their bases. For the present, however, we must be content with the materials at hand.

Table 24 shows the relationship between the new composite index and scientific orientations among the sample of faculty members. In accord with the previous findings, we note that scientific orientations are highest among those scored lowest on the free-will image-of-man index, and those scientific orientations decrease steadily as we move across the table in the direction of a greater commitment to the traditional image.

TABLE 24

FREE-WILL IMAGE-OF-MAN INDEX AND
SCIENTIFIC ORIENTATIONS

	Free-Will Image-of-Man Index						
	Low 0	1	2	3	4	5	High 6
Percentage scientists	83	79	69	67	54	49	44
	(18)	(42)	(65)	(81)	(84)	(72)	(18)

Note: Number in parentheses represents number of cases on which percentage is based.

Summary and Conclusions

This chapter had advanced the thesis that the rise of science in medicine is related to an overall shift in American morality. It was suggested that the traditional, individualistic morality, based on a belief in each man's total control over his destiny, is being steadily replaced by a more deterministic view of man as a product of his environment. Scientific orientations, it was suggested, are based on an acceptance of determinism, which should have a greater affinity for the new morality than for the old.

The empirical analyses confirmed the thesis. Commitment to the traditional religious and political perspectives were found to be incompatible with science. Moreover, those same traditional perspectives were found to support the traditional image of man as a free-will agent, when two attitudinal items were introduced. Finally, faculty members holding the free-will image of man were less scientifically oriented than those who held the new deterministic image. It was concluded, therefore, that the rise of medical science is part of a general shift in social morality.

Since the new social morality at least partly releases man from the strict accountability so basic to the individualistic morality, we must now ask whether the change in morality generally has any significant effects on medical morality as represented by the traditional norms of humane patient care. It is this question to which we now turn.

CHAPTER FOUR

Science, Morality, and Patient Care

In chapter two, it was discovered that scientific faculty members were no more nor less committed to the traditional norms of humane patient care than were the nonscientific faculty. As subsequent analyses have shown, however, science and morality are not irrelevant to one another. Indeed, the rise of scientific medicine coincides with the decline of a traditional American morality: that based on individual responsibility.

In now turning to an examination of the effects of the new social morality on the norms of compassion, responsibility, and respect for experimental subjects, we might have two possible expectations. First, the new image of man as a product of his environment might lead faculty members to ignore the traditional concerns. If man is deprived of the individual freedom and responsibility which were formerly attributed to him, can a physician be expected to show the same amount of respect for him as a total human being? It might be expected, therefore, that faculty members committed to the new morality would be less concerned with the traditional norms.

At the same time, there are grounds for believing that the new morality provides alternative grounds for humane patient care. We have already noted that in the areas of poverty, deviance, and Negro civil rights, the new morality appears more compassionate, more sympathetic to suffering. The pejorative term "bleeding heart" is not altogether inaccurate. Perhaps, then, faculty members committed to the new social morality are generally more sympathetic and would exhibit that sympathy in their dealings with patients. If this were the case, the new social morality would not constitute a threat to the traditional norms of humane patient care. It might indeed strengthen commitment to them.

We shall turn now to an empirical examination of these two possibilities. We shall reconsider faculty members' responses to the items measuring compassion, responsibility, and respect for experimental subjects, taking into account both their scientific and their moral orientations.

Compassion, Science, and Morality

It will be recalled that faculty members in the present survey were asked how they would treat the surviving family of a non-private ward patient who had died. They were given the choice of speaking to the surviving family themselves or delegating this task to members of the house staff. Speaking to the family personally was taken as an indication of greater compassion on the faculty member's part than delegating the duty to someone else.

In the earlier analysis, scientific and nonscientific faculty members did not differ significantly in their responses to the question. It was concluded, therefore, than science does not constitute a threat to compassion in patient care. Now we must ask if the new social morality constitutes such a threat.

Table 25 is an examination of faculty responses to this item in terms of scores on the new free-will image-of-man index.

TABLE 25

RESPONSES TO PATIENT'S DEATH—BY THE
FREE-WILL IMAGE-OF-MAN INDEX

Question: Would you personally speak to the surviving family,
or would you delegate this duty to the house staff?

	Free-Will Image-of-Man Index						
	Low						High
	0	1	2	3	4	5	6
Percentage who would speak to the surviving family at least as a general rule	42	36	35	31	28	26	26
	(19)	(44)	(68)	(84)	(90)	(73)	(19)

Note: Number in parentheses represents number of cases on which percentage is based.

If anything, it would appear that the new social morality—
represented by the deterministic image of man—is more compassionate in this circumstance than is the traditional, individualistic morality. Forty-two percent of those scored lowest on
the free-will index say they would personally speak to the surviving family. The percentage decreases steadily as we move
across the table. Among those most committed to the traditional image of man as a free-will agent, only 26 percent say
they would speak to the family.

We should recognize that the percentage-point difference
in this case is rather small in view of the range of index scores.
One would hardly conclude that the new social morality is
bringing about a revolution in compassionate patient care.
Nonetheless, the observed relationship is strong and consistent
enough to justify a more modest conclusion in that regard. At
the very least, the new morality does not undermine the compassion expected of physicians any more than science does.
Rather it provides a support for compassionate behavior at

least as substantial as that provided by the traditional morality which it is replacing.

The fact that the new morality appears more compassionate and humane in other areas of life (e.g., poverty) should increase our confidence in the validity of the present finding. It seems likely, though by no means certain, that more rigorous future examinations of the new morality and patient care will substantiate our present, tentative conclusion.

TABLE 26

SPEAKING TO SURVIVORS—BY SCIENTIFIC ORIENTATIONS
AND FREE-WILL IMAGE-OF-MAN INDEX

Percentage who would at least generally speak to the surviving family

Free-Will Image-of-Man Index	Index of Scientific Orientations			
	Low 0	1	2	High 3
Low: 0–2	* (7)	24 (25)	35 (52)	41 (41)
Medium: 3–4	32 (19)	24 (46)	33 (61)	32 (38)
High: 5–6	15 (13)	32 (34)	26 (23)	25 (20)

Note: Number in parentheses represents number of cases on which percentage is based.
* Too few cases for a stable percentage.

In another sense, the latest finding presents a puzzle. We recall from the earlier examination that scientific orientations were not related to compassion. The new social morality, however, is related to both compassion and scientific orientations. It will be useful, therefore, to examine the joint effects of science and morality on compassion. Table 26 does this.

Unfortunately, the small size of the present sample of faculty members does not permit a complete analysis of this question. Yet, by combining scores on the free-will index, it is possible to get an impression of the trivariate relationship.

Faculty members scored highest on scientific orientations and lowest on the free-will image of man are the most compassionate (41 percent). At the other extreme, those most committed to the free-will image and least committed to science are the least compassionate (15 percent). Between these extremes the picture is more ambiguous. Nevertheless, some patterns may be noted.

With the exception of those scored *1* on scientific orientations, the negative relationship between compassion and the free-will image of man is maintained. This is most clearly seen among the most scientific faculty. More important, however, these new data fill out our understanding of the influence of science as such.

Among faculty members most committed to the new social morality (scored low on the free-will index), compassion increases with science. Under these conditions, then, scientific medicine has just the opposite effect from what its critics suggest. Turning to those most committed to the free-will image, and discounting for the moment those scored lowest on science, the relationship is somewhat reversed. Within the framework of the traditional, individualistic morality, science somewhat decreases faculty compassion. When scientific orientations are combined with the new social morality, however, the opposite occurs.

These initial findings provide a tentative impression of the joint effects of science and morality on compassion. The nature of the indicators and the ambiguities apparent in the empirical relationships should caution the reader to withhold his final conclusions on the matter until more evidence has been introduced.

Responsibility, Science, and Morality

In chapter two, two items were introduced as indicators of faculty responsibility for patients assigned them in the university hospital. Both items measured the degree of personal supervision exercised by faculty over the house staff members who assisted them in patient care. In the earlier analysis, it was found that scientific orientations did not affect faculty responses on these items.

The traditional, individualistic morality was based on a belief that each individual was responsible for his own actions. In this sense, a man's success or failure was a mark of his inner worth. It might also be said that the traditional morality produced a rhetoric of responsibility. A "sense of responsibility" was a highly valued quality, and the irresponsible man was looked down upon much as was the failure. It might be the case, therefore, that the decline of the traditional morality would represent an easing up on responsibility in this sense. Faculty members holding the new social morality therefore might be the less rigorous in their exercise of personal responsibility.

At the same time, the new social morality has a rhetoric of responsibility. In various contexts, it is suggested that society as a whole is responsible (guilty) for the suffering of its individual members and that the society must accept responsibility (obligation) for alleviating the suffering which exists. It is argued that the poor are poor because of the general social structure and because of the actions of the wealthy. Thus the more fortunate members of the society are obliged to help the less fortunate. This represents a different conception of responsibility, however, and its implications for face-to-face medical situation are unclear.

Table 27 presents faculty responses to the question regard-

TABLE 27

HOUSE STAFF SUPERVISION—BY FREE-WILL
IMAGE-OF-MAN INDEX

	Free-Will Image-of-Man Index						
	Low						High
	0	1	2	3	4	5	6
Percentage who required the house staff to report daily at a specified time	64	71	60	56	56	51	54
	(11)	(31)	(35)	(55)	(64)	(45)	(13)

Note: Number in parentheses represents number of cases on which percentage is based.

ing the manner in which their house staff assistants reported to them on the care of patients. Under each score on the free-will image-of-man index, the percentage saying the house staff reported to them at a specified time every day is shown. We note that the relationship between morality and responsibility is far less clear than in the preceding examination of compassion. Overall, faculty committed to the new morality (scored low on free will) are somewhat more likely to report close supervision of the house staff, but the effect of the index is neither strong nor consistent.

The lack of clarity in these data is not alleviated when we consider the second indicator of responsibility. The reader will recall that faculty members were asked the procedure by which major therapeutic and diagnostic decisions were made regarding their patients while they themselves were not on duty. Faculty who said they were called in personally to make the decisions were adjudged the most responsible, but this response was not related to scientific orientations. Table 28 indicates that morality does not provide a clear answer to faculty differences either.

TABLE 28

OFF-DUTY DECISIONS BY FREE-WILL IMAGE-OF-MAN INDEX

	Free-Will Image-of-Man Index						
	Low 0	1	2	3	4	5	High 6
Percentage who made the major off-duty decisions themselves	7 (14)	33 (27)	48 (42)	37 (54)	42 (66)	48 (44)	25 (12)

Note: Number in parentheses represents number of cases on which percentage is based.

If we look only at the two extreme index scores in table 28, it appears that the free-will image of man is more conducive to responsibility in this instance than is the deterministic image. This conclusion proves unfounded, however, when we examine the intermediate index scores. Indeed, the percentage reporting that they made the major off-duty decisions themselves changes across-the-index scores in such a way as to produce no consistent pattern. Both tables 27 and 28 suggest that faculty members' acceptance of the new or the old moralities has no significant effect on responsibility.

Table 29 examines the joint effects of science and morality on faculty supervision of the house staff. This new table largely matches the previous findings of no relationships. However, one aspect of the table should be noted. The scientific faculty (3 on scientific orientations) who still retain their commitments to the free-will image of man are the least likely to have the house staff report daily at a specified time. Only 36 percent gave this response, compared with from 54 to 71 percent of the other faculty groups. Among these most scientific faculty, responsibility increases steadily as we move up the column in the direction of the new social morality, based on a deterministic image of man. Somewhat the same finding holds for faculty scored *2* on scientific orientations.

TABLE 29

HOUSE STAFF SUPERVISION—BY SCIENTIFIC ORIENTATIONS
AND FREE-WILL IMAGE-OF-MAN INDEX

Percentage who required house staff to report daily at a specified time

Free-Will Image-of-Man Index	Index of Scientific Orientations		
	Low 0 + 1*	2	High 3
Low: 0–2	71 (21)	63 (32)	65 (23)
Medium: 3–4	54 (48)	58 (45)	55 (20)
High: 5–6	57 (28)	56 (18)	36 (11)

Note: Number in parentheses represents number of cases on which percentage is based.
* Scores of *0* and *1* have been combined in this table because of the small number of faculty members in the lowest category. The reduction in the number of cases is due to the limitation of this table to faculty members who were assigned patients in the university hospital.

This minor pattern in table 29 takes on more significance when we recall that essentially the same pattern was found in the examination of compassion, earlier. The combination of science and the free-will image of man may possibly threaten the traditional norms of humane patient care. We shall return to this point after more data have been introduced.

Table 30 presents an examination of the joint effects of science and morality on the other indicator of patient responsibility: procedures for making major off-duty decisions regarding hospital patients. This table provides even less information than the preceding one. In each row of the table, faculty members scored lowest on scientific orientations are the most responsible, yet those scored highest are consistently second in this regard. The most responsible faculty in the table are those lowest on scientific orientations and most committed to the free-will image of man, but they do not fit into any overall pattern of relationships.

TABLE 30

OFF-DUTY DECISIONS—BY SCIENTIFIC ORIENTATIONS
AND FREE-WILL IMAGE-OF-MAN INDEX

Percentage who made the major off-duty decisions themselves

Free-Will Image-of-Man Index	Index of Scientific Orientations		
	Low 0 + 1	2	High 3
Low: 0–2	45 (22)	34 (29)	36 (28)
Medium: 3–4	42 (43)	36 (45)	38 (24)
High: 5–6	57 (26)	31 (13)	38 (16)

Note: Number in parentheses represents number of cases on which percentage is based.

On the whole, it seems safest to conclude that there is no relationship between science and morality, on the one hand, and responsible patient care, on the other. This is not to deny that some relationships might appear in an analysis utilizing better indicators than are available to the present study. However, within the limits of the present data, there is no warrant for predicting that such relationships would appear.

Human Experimentation, Science, and Morality

In this final section, we shall examine the joint effects of science and morality on faculty attitudes regarding human experimentation. We recall that respondents to the survey were asked whether they felt an experimenter was obligated to participate as a subject in a dangerous experiment involving healthy human subjects. This was taken as an indication of his respect for the worth of his subjects' lives, and it was discovered that scientific orientations did not affect the responses given.

In turning to the implications of morality for this issue, two contradictory expectations are warranted. First, for reasons discussed on several occasions above, the new social morality, based on a deterministic image of man, potentially denies the idiosyncratic significance of the individual. It denies his individual accountability for his actions and regards him as the convergence of several variables rather than as an integral whole. It would be reasonable to suppose therefore that faculty members committed to the new social morality might be less likely to support the experimenter's obligation to his subjects to share their risks.

On the other hand, another aspect of the new social morality would suggest a greater support for the experimenter's obligation to participate. The new social morality, especially in its prescriptions for social change, reflects the basic American value of equality. The differential achievements observed among men are attributed, not to their inner worth, but to the social environment which shapes them. The programs of social action proposed as part of the new social morality all point in the direction of a greater democratization. The poor, for example, are considered to suffer poverty through no fault of their own, and the thrust of the new social morality is toward greater social action to eradicate the poverty which exists. From this perspective, the poor *deserve* physical comforts as much as the rich.

One might expect therefore that the democratic element of the new social morality would support democratic participation in dangerous experiments. We will recall from chapter two that many of the arguments in support of experimenter participation were based on the principles of democracy: the experimenter was deemed no more valuable as a human being than were his experimental subjects. Hence, the new social morality may lead to a greater support for experimenter participation.

Table 31 presents the relationship between morality and faculty responses to the question regarding experimenter participation. It will be recalled that many faculty members wrote in answers to this question rather than simply selecting one of the answers provided in the questionnaire. In view of this, the table presents six answer categories rather than just the three originally offered.

TABLE 31

EXPERIMENTER PARTICIPATION—BY FREE-WILL
IMAGE-OF-MAN INDEX

Question: Should the experimenter participate in his own dangerous experiments?	Free-Will Image-of-Man Index						
	Low						High
	0	1	2	3	4	5	6
Moral obligation to participate	12%	26%	23%	33%	24%	17%	19%
Generally unwise to participate	44	49	57	46	62	54	69
Should be prohibited	19	2	4	9	5	14	6
Experimenter should decide*	6	10	6	6	7	3	6
Experimenter should be willing*	0	5	5	1	1	4	0
Should not experiment*	19	8	5	5	1	8	0
100% =	(16)	(39)	(65)	(80)	(81)	(66)	(16)

Note: Number in parentheses represents number of cases on which percentage is based.
* These responses were volunteered by respondents.

The data in table 31 do not point to any consistent relationship between morality and experimenter participation. Neither the new nor the old morality appears to encourage support for democratic participation in dangerous experiments. While the profiles of responses shown for the several index scores differ from one another in certain particulars, there is no discernible pattern.

We must tentatively conclude that neither does the new social morality lead faculty members to lose respect for the human worth of experimental subjects, nor, contrariwise, does it lead them to a greater support for democratic participation. It, like science, appears to have no significant effect.

Let us turn now to an examination of the joint effects of science and morality on this issue. Although neither has an overall effect, the previous analyses have shown that they may have a combined effect. Table 32 groups faculty members by their scientific orientations and their scores on the free-will image-of-man index. The percentages represent those faculty members who either said the experimenter has a moral obligation to participate, volunteered the answer that the experimenter should be willing to participate, or volunteered the response that dangerous experiments should not be conducted on healthy subjects. All three of these responses seem to represent a concern for the human worth of the experimental subjects, which is the primary variable being examined here. For this reason, it makes more sense to combine the three responses. (It should be noted, however, that the pattern of responses shown in table 32 is virtually identical to that produced when only the three original responses are examined and percentages represent those saying the experimenter is morally obligated to participate.)

The most striking observation to be made in table 32 concerns those faculty members scored high on scientific orientations and high in their commitment to the traditional, free-will image of man. They are the least likely of all faculty members to express concern for the human worth of experimental subjects. This finding should bring to mind corresponding discoveries with regard to compassion and responsibility.

TABLE 32

EXPERIMENTER PARTICIPATION—BY SCIENTIFIC
ORIENTATIONS AND FREE-WILL
IMAGE-OF-MAN INDEX

Percentage concerned for the human worth of experimental subjects*

Free-Will Image-of-Man Index	Index of Scientific Orientations			
	Low 0	1	2	High 3
Low: 0–2	† (5)	29 (24)	39 (49)	32 (38)
Medium: 3–4	17 (18)	27 (41)	38 (58)	35 (34)
High: 5–6	36 (11)	41 (32)	20 (20)	6 (18)

* Since a number of faculty members volunteered their own responses to this question, it seems valuable to take those into account here. The percentages shown in this table represent those faculty who said the experimenter had a moral obligation to participate in his own experiments, plus those who volunteered responses saying he should be willing to participate and those who objected to dangerous experiments on human beings.

† Too few cases for a stable percentage.

Looking at the rest of the table, there is little more to be said. Considering those faculty scored 2 and 3 on scientific orientations, we note something of an increase in concern for experimental subjects as we move up the columns toward the deterministic image of man. Among the two groups scored lower on scientific orientations, the overall relationship is in the opposite direction. While there is the hint of an interaction between science and morality in shaping faculty concerns for experimental subjects, it is not strongly demonstrated by the present data. In this regard, the latest tables support the earlier ones in this chapter in suggesting that the rise of the new social morality is not having a significant effect on traditional norms of humane patient-physician relations.

Summary and Conclusions

The purpose of this chapter has been similar to that of chapter two: to examine the prospects for humane patient care in the future of American medicine. Where chapter two examined the possible influence of scientific orientations, the present one has focused on the new social morality, based on a more deterministic image of man. Chapter two concluded that science does not threaten the traditional norms; the present one offers essentially the same conclusion regarding the new social morality.

Overall, faculty members committed to the new social morality are slightly more compassionate than those who remain committed to the individualistic morality. The relationship is not especially strong, but it is consistent. At the very least, it may be concluded that the new social morality provides as much support for compassion as does the old morality.

When the analysis turned to the issue of patient responsibility, there was no discernible effect of morality on faculty supervision of house staff members or on their procedures for the making of major decision during their off-duty hours. Again, the new and the old moralities offer equally good (or poor) support for responsible patient care. The rise of the new social morality does not seem to threaten that norm.

Finally, it was discovered that the two moralities are essentially irrelevant to faculty concerns for experimental subjects. The individualistic morality, based on the inherent worth of each individual human being, does not provide greater concern; neither does the new social morality, with its emphasis on democratic principles, have this effect. Again, it must be concluded that the rise of the new social morality does not represent a trend toward more inhumanity in medical research.

It is anticipated that many readers will find these conclusions as unsatisfactory as those of chapter two. It might be argued that the indicators of humane patient care used in these analyses are not adequate to the research problem. There is certainly much merit in this criticism, and the conclusions drawn here must remain tentative until later research can replicate them through the use of better measures. At the same time, the consistency of the findings across all indicators should cause the reader to entertain the possibility that the future of medical care is less gloomy than he might have imagined.

When future research is conducted with regard to the issues just examined here, consideration should be given to another of the tentative conclusions drawn in the present study. There are reasons to suspect that scientific faculty members who still retain a commitment to the traditional individualistic morality are the least committed to the traditional norms of humane patient care. The analyses in this chapter showed them to be relatively low in compassion, responsibility, and concern for human experimental subjects.

The concluding remarks in chapter two spoke of the distinction between cognitive and affective modes, distinguishing humanism from humanitarianism. While the present data do not permit an elaboration of this theme, there are reasons for believing that the new social morality represents a greater degree of humanitarianism. In the context of social action, it appears more sympathetic to human suffering than was the traditional morality which stressed the individual's personal responsibility for his life situation.

The analyses in this chapter at least hold open the possibility that science potentially threatens humane social relations, but that scientific medical faculty members are linked to the new social morality by virtue of a shared emphasis on determinism, and the humanitarian aspect of the new morality may prevent their scientific orientations from making them less humane. Those faculty members who do not accept the new social morality do not have this check against the potential scientific threat to humane social relations. Thus, when scientific faculty retain commitments to the traditional free-will image of man, they appear less humane in their dealings with patients.

This conclusion is especially tentative. The data available to the present study cannot begin to provide a rigorous test. Nevertheless, the hint of an interaction between science and morality is evident, and the long-range significance of the suggested relationship warrants a more rigorous examination in the future. Such future studies should devote more careful attention to examining the kinds of scientific orientations found among those scientists committed to the free-will and deterministic images of man. Whereas scientific explanation is basically deterministic, scientists who accept the free-will image of man may conceivably limit their scientific concerns to matters of description rather than explanation. This and other possibilities ought to be explored more carefully.

Finally, it will be necessary to elaborate the mechanisms whereby cognitive and affective orientations come to influence humane relations among man. The preceding analyses have done little more than describe the existence or absence of these effects. Future research must delineate the manner in which they operate.

PART THREE

Prospects for the Future

INTRODUCTION TO PART THREE

Parts one and two have examined the effects of contemporary changes in American medicine on the traditional norms of humane patient-physician relations. In answer to our initial inquiry, it was discovered that scientific orientations do not appear to pose a threat to such traditional norms as compassion, responsibility, and respect for human life. The most recent analyses have pointed to the rise of a new social morality in American society which is associated with the rise of science in American medicine. Yet even the new morality, alone or in conjunction with science, cannot be said to threaten the traditional norms that have been examined in this study.

At the same time, it would be foolhardy to conclude that the new social morality—based on a deterministic image of man—will have no effect on medicine in the long run. There are good reasons to believe it will have very important effects, even in addition to its facilitation of scientific orientations. Although the new social morality does not appear to threaten the patient-physician relationship in the terms examined in this book so far, it does hold significant implications for the nature of that relationship.

Surely one of the more salient effects of the new social morality has to do with the conditions under which medical care ought to be provided. Traditionally, American medical care has been provided on a fee-for-service basis, whereby the patient agrees to reimburse the physician for his professional efforts. This system has been an integral part of the individualistic morality which has been discussed above. The physician has been held personally responsible for providing his services to his patients, and the patients, in turn, have been held personally responsible for paying.

The new social morality represents a challenge to this system. Basing their case on the value of equality and a deterministic image of man, the proponents of the new social morality speak of the right to medical care, based on medical need, just as they speak of the right to food, shelter, education, and so forth. Denying that man's life situation is his own total responsibility, they argue that the provision of medical care according to the ability to pay for it is immoral. (According to the individualistic morality, of course, the person who couldn't or wouldn't pay for medical care was to be judged immoral or at least lacking in inner strength and worth.)

The notion that everyone has a right to medical care is not a new one. It may be found appearing at several points in medical history. The varied and sometimes ambiguous history of this notion is instructive to the present examination.

Although Americans are more familiar with the fee-for-service system of medicine, it is by no means the most common type of arrangement. At the dawn of medicine, we find physicians employed on a salary basis to provide their services to a given population. Sigerist notes, for example, that many of the best physicians of ancient Egypt were retained in the palaces of the royal families. Others were employed to accompany the armies and labor parties.[1] Thus, for an established salary, the physicians provided whatever services were needed to whomever needed them within the specified population. Undoubtedly, a similar form of arrangement characterized the priest-physicians of the other Mesopotamian civilizations. Later, in the Roman Empire, physicians were employed by the government to care for slaves.[2] And in medieval Europe, the cleric-physicians were subsisted by the Church, rather than by the fees obtained from their patients.

The exact origins of free *public* medical care are uncertain. In 1880, a French physician, A. Vercoutre, challenged the prevailing belief that the Romans had been the prime innovators in this area by suggesting that the Greek city-states had provided free medical care to all citizens through the employment of "public physicians." [3] In the years that followed, many writers joined in the discussion, attempting to assess the validity of Vercoutre's contention.

In a more recent historical examination, Louis Cohn-Haft concludes that the Greek city-states did not provide the free medical care attributed to them.[4] Rather, his researches indicate that various physicians were honored for volunteering free medical care on occasion and that the city-states sometimes provided stipends to certain physicians as a means of insuring their presence in the city. He feels it is unlikely that physicians were totally reimbursed by the government so they could provide free care to all citizens of the city.

This example provides an early indication of the primary ambiguity regarding the right to medical care. While Ver-

1. Henry E. Sigerist, *A History of Medicine* (New York: Oxford University Press, 1951), pp. 320ff.
2. This represented the origin of hospitals, as well.
3. A. Vercoutre, "La Médicine Publique dans L'antiquité Grecque," *Revue Archéologique*, n.s. 39 (1880); cited by Louis Cohn-Haft in *The Public Physicians of Ancient Greece*, Smith College Studies in History, vol. 42 (1956), p. 1.
4. Louis Cohn-Haft, *Public Physicians.*

coutre suggests that the Greeks showed a commitment to the belief that everyone inherently deserved medical care, Cohn-Haft's interpretation represents the compromise principle which has been common in medicine of all eras: that physicians have an obligation to offer gratuitous medical care sometimes. Thus for example, in the Hippocratic *Precepts,* the private practitioners of ancient Greece were enjoined "not to be too grasping, but to consider carefully your patient's means. Sometimes give your services for nothing." [5] Similarly, the *AMA Principles of 1912* support the spirit of the Hippocratic injunction: "The poverty of the patient . . . should command the gratuitous services of the physician." [6]

Implicit in such statements is the view that medical care is basically a quantity that is for sale to those who desire it, but that the physician may choose to offer it gratuitously as an altruistic gesture. This view should not be confused, however, with the view of medical care as a basic human right.

Whatever the situation in the Greek city-states discussed above, Sigerist suggests that the primary source of the view that medical care is a human right is to be found in the medical profession of the Middle Ages in Europe.[7] Then, surgeons were considered to be craftsmen, but the majority of physicians were clerics, employed and supported by the Church. As salaried physicians, they were in a position to offer their services without charge to all those in need of them. There can be no doubt that the ability to provide medical care to the rich and poor alike was further strengthened by the ethics of Christianity, which suggested that all men—as God's children—deserved the gift of health and life. Thus, we find the administration of

5. Quoted by Douglas Guthrie in *A History of Medicine* (Philadelphia: J. B. Lippincott Co., 1946), p. 54.
6. Chapter II, Article VI, Sect. 1.
7. The following discussion is based on Henry Sigerist, *Medicine and Human Welfare* (New Haven: Yale University Press, 1947), especially pp. 118–122.

medical care as a religious mission, and that the practitioners of the time were performing a religious duty.

The medical ethic of the medieval cleric-physicians, then, was a religious ethic; healing was a religious mission. This ethic was evident in the Christian adaptation of the hospital as an institution for healing. Garrison calls the organization of hospitals and sick-nursing "the chief glory of medieval medicine" and attributes much of this glory to Christianity: "The spirit of antiquity toward sickness and misfortune was not one of compassion, and the credit of ministering to human suffering on an extended scale belongs to Christianity." [8] The earliest Christian hospitals were established to provide for the care of the poor and others who might not be able to obtain private medical care. "These eventually became specialized, according to Christian ideas of the obligations of charity and hospitality, as: Nosocomia or claustral hospitals, for the reception and care of the sick alone; Brephotrophia, for foundlings; Orphanotrophia for orphans; Ptochia, for the helpless poor; Gerontochia, for the aged; and Xenodochia, for poor and infirm pilgrims." [9]

The strength of this ethic supporting medical care as a human right may be seen best in the context of the social changes which marked the end of the Middle Ages and of the static medieval culture. From about the eleventh century, increasing numbers of laymen entered medicine, and since they were not supported by the Church, many entered into private practice on a fee-for-service basis. Still, even at this point, most sought salaried positions in the employ of government or secular hospitals. For the lay practitioner, the norms of professional conduct were largely informed by the same religious ethic noted above.

8. Fielding H. Garrison, *An Introduction to the History of Medicine* (Philadelphia: W. B. Saunders Co., 1929), p. 176.
9. *Ibid.*, p. 177.

Around the sixteenth century, however, an economic and religious revolution began to take place. As discussed in part two, Weber and others have examined the rise of the Protestant ethic of hard work and observable achievement, which laid the grounds for economic expansion and the rise of competitive capitalism.[10] Rather than seeking salvation through the proper exercise of one's station in life, men began to seek the evidence of salvation in the form of worldly success. Basically, the ethic which informed ascetic Protestantism held that every man should work hard in his occupation (or calling), but— opposed to the medieval scheme—material success was an indication of how diligently he followed his calling. The resultant norm, therefore, was not service qua service, but service for pecuniary gain. This new ethic influenced most occupations.

Physicians, however, resisted the new order of things, and their continued resistance is indicative of the sanctity of their medieval ethic. The religious belief that all men deserved medical care, whether or not they could afford to pay, did not die easily. Physicians continued to seek salaried positions so that they could provide their services to all without having to compromise their principles for material gain. Sigerist notes that as late as the end of the nineteenth century, many European physicians had never sent out a bill for services.[11] Instead, they attempted to provide their services to the members of a village or to a group of families. At Christmas, the patients sent whatever they could afford to the physician. While such physicians did not make a lot of money, they continued to view their profession as a religious calling and continued to believe that all men had a right to medical care.

Despite the strength of the ethic which grew out of medieval

10. Max Weber, *The Protestant Ethic and the Spirit of Capitalism*, trans. Talcott Parsons (New York: Charles Scribner's Sons, 1958); and see, for example, R. H. Tawney, *Religion and the Rise of Capitalism* (New York: Harcourt, Brace & Co., 1926).
11. Sigerist, *Medicine and Human Welfare*, pp. 118ff.

medicine, this profession, like others, has become a business. The fee-for-service system of remuneration has predominated throughout most of American medical history.[12] Although the American medical profession has been encouraged to be charitable and provide some gratuitous care, as noted earlier, the American Medical Association has been at least as explicit in placing limits on such orientations. Having suggested that physicians should take their patient's poverty into account, the *AMA Principles of 1912* immediately added: "But institutions endowed by societies, the organizations for mutual benefit, or for accident, sickness and life insurance, or for analogous purposes, should be accorded no such privilege."[13] The intent of this statement is made clearer when we turn to the *AMA Code of Ethics of 1847.* "A wealthy physician should not give advice *gratis* to the affluent; because his doing so is an injury to his professional brethren. The office of a physician can never be supported as an exclusively beneficent one; and it is defrauding, in some degree, the common funds for its support, when fees are dispensed with which might justly be claimed."[14]

Statements such as these clearly point to the radical difference between the orientations of medieval medicine and recent American medicine. Despite occasional allowances for gratuitous care, American medicine is a business, and it is no exaggeration to say that the profession has exhibited an inordinate concern for its own interest.[15] This orientation in American

12. The travel expenses of many of the early physicians coming to the American colonies were paid by the various colonial governments or the commercial firms who founded the colonies. Some also received stipends for serving a given area, but their services were nonetheless paid for predominantly by their patients.
13. Chapter II, Article VI, Sect. 1.
14. Chapter II, Art. V, Para. 9.
15. Take for example the *AMA Principles of 1912*. Five sections are devoted to the topic "The Duties of Physicians to their Patients," another 4 concern "The Duties of the Profession to the Public," while the remaining 31 sections deal with "The Duties of Physicians to Each Other and to the Profession at Large."

medicine is, as noted above, in harmony with the traditional, individualistic morality of American society. Like any other businessman, the physician must take care of himself, look out for his own interests. The patient, in turn, is expected to do the same. If the physician cannot practice or the patient cannot afford medical care, it is basically their own fault.

The new social morality, however, represents a threat to this orientation in medicine as elsewhere. The new morality represents a return to the medieval ethic in medicine, to the belief that everyone has a basic human right to medical care if he is in need of it. As a practical matter, no one has suggested that physicians assume vows of poverty in order to act out this ethic. Instead, the thrust of activity has been in the direction of government financing of medical care. In its extreme, this is the "socialized medicine" which the American medical community has fought bitterly for years. More immediately, the new morality has produced moderate programs of medical care to special, deprived groups. The best-known program is Medical Care for the Aged, or Medicare.

This rather lengthy account of the notion of medical care as a human right has been presented because it undoubtedly represents the most salient, immediate effect of the new social morality. Chapter five, which follows, presents an examination of faculty members' attitudes toward Medicare. The findings of that examination provide empirical evidence of the impact of the new social morality.

At the same time, the examination of Medicare points to an even more basic phenomenon, one which transcends even the new social morality. It is apparent that we are entering an era of rapid and perhaps radical change in the structure of medicine. The new social morality and its belief in a deterministic nature of man provides only one example of the unprecedented breaking down of tradition. Norms and values which have been accepted for decades and centuries are now being reconsidered and potentially restructured. During such a period of change, we must ask how the new structures in medicine will be built. What motives, what value-orientations shape medical opinions on the desired organization of tomorrow's medicine?

The most general conclusion to be drawn from the examination of attitudes toward Medicare is that faculty members, and one might assume physicians in general, formed their personal opinions on the basis of broad, social orientations—not medical orientations. In chapter five we shall see that attitudes toward Medicare bear no relationship to faculty members' medical orientations and medical experiences. Their commitments to the old and the new social moralities provide the only relevant source of attitudes on this issue.

Chapter six, in a rather short analysis, confirms this general conclusion in another context. Faculty members were asked to report their attitudes regarding a hypothetical case of infanticide. Some were unalterably opposed, while others seemed willing to support it, in some cases at least. The source of their differences, however, was not to be found in their medical orientations. Only their religious orientations, this time, provide the answer.

These findings suggest caution as we enter this era of changing medical structures and values. On medical issues, one is tempted to accept the testimony of physicians as being especially relevant. Yet the findings of chapters five and six indicate that such "expert" testimony is based on the same broad social orientations which inform the attitudes of laymen. The issue of medical care as a human right is a social issue, not a medical one, and physicians as well as laymen form their attitudes in terms of social morality, not specifically medical morality. The same may be said for issues such as infanticide, abortions, prepaid medical insurance, socialized medicine, and so forth.

CHAPTER FIVE

The Right to Medical Care

The preceding introduction has traced, in part, the history of the notion that medical care is a human right, not a commercial service to be purchased by those in need. We have also seen that the individualistic morality of America's past conflicted with the notion of medical care as a right. In terms of the traditional morality, the physician and his patient were responsible, as individuals, for making the necessary arrangements for the provision and reimbursement of professional services.

The new social morality, however, suggests that medical care should, once again, be regarded as a basic human right. Just as the new morality holds the impoverished largely blameless for their poverty and suggests that the society is obligated to provide for their needs, it also suggests that the individual is not to blame for becoming ill or for being unable to pay for medical care. It is suggested, therefore, that medical care should be provided on the basis of medical need, rather than on the basis of ability to pay.

This chapter examines medical school faculty members' attitudes regarding Medicare. At the time of the survey, the program had been enacted by Congress, but had not gone into effect. We shall examine faculty support and opposition on this issue, first in terms of their medical orientations and activities, and then in terms of their images of man as measured by the composite index constructed in chapter three.

The purposes of this examination are twofold. First, it provides intrinsically interesting information about the sources of support and opposition regarding this significant program. Second, and more important, it provides an example of the manner in which physicians form opinions on the kind of sociomedical issue which is appearing more and more frequently in the present day.

The Debate over Medicare

Elsewhere in the world—in Britain, Australia, the Scandinavian countries, the Soviet-bloc nations, and others—governments have established national health-care programs which insure access to medical treatment for all citizens. In some cases, the services are completely free, while in others, minimal fees are charged of patients. These programs are under the sponsorship of the national governments and are offset by government revenues. In the United States, the function of such national programs has been performed primarily by employee health plans, voluntary prepayment programs such as Blue Cross, and by institutional health-care organizations such as the Kaiser Foundation Health Plan. Still, the topic of national health insurance is not unknown to Americans.

In 1949, President Harry S. Truman sought passage of a national health-insurance program similar to those existing in Europe. The proposed legislation brought much of the medical community to its feet in angry protest. Dr. Louis H. Bauer called it "an extreme example of compulsory paternalism . . . contrary to our established ways and habits of life and political principles." [1] Charges of "socialized medicine" flew freely. In the end the measure was defeated.

In the ensuing years, efforts to obtain a national health program took a more piecemeal form. In particular, attention focused on plans which would provide free medical care for the elderly. It was contended that older Americans present the most desperate medical need. The savings of a lifetime were deemed insufficient to take care of the rising costs of medical care, or even the costs of voluntary prepayment plans. On October 1, 1960, the Kerr-Mills Medical Assistance for the Aged (MAA) act took effect.

Enactment of the Kerr-Mills program again raised protests from the medical community. In an article entitled, "Socialized Medicine? We've got it in Kerr-Mills," Dr. Fred A. Marx wrote that nonparticipation in the program was a "hollow freedom. . . . It pits the lone private practitioner against the toughest most tamper-proof monopoly going—Government monopoly.

". . . If the doctor can't tolerate the consequences of nonparticipation, his remaining choice is to participate. When he does, he's tied to the State in all Kerr-Mills dealings, just as surely as if he were on the State's payroll!" [2] On the whole, however, the reaction to Kerr-Mills was mild in comparison with that experienced earlier by Truman. The American Medical Association even purchased advertising in support of the measure.

The Kerr-Mills program was not enough in the eyes of many proponents of government action in medical care. Federal assistance was dependent on the initiative of the individual states.

1. Louis Bauer in testimony before a subcommittee of the Committee on Labor and Public Welfare on May 25, 1949, quoted in "The Federal Government's Role in Providing Medical Care to Citizens of the United States," Education and Public Welfare Division of the Legislative Reference Service, Library of Congress (Washington: U.S. Government Printing Office, 1963), p. 11.
2. Fred A. Marx, "Socialized Medicine? We've got it in Kerr-Mills," *Medical Economics*, April 22, 1963, pp. 178, 180.

As a result, both the extent and quality of administering the program varied from state to state. The greatest objection voiced by the proponents of government action centered on the program's eligibility requirements. Kerr-Mills was designed to assist those elderly people who were deemed unable to provide for their own medical needs. While the goal seemed reasonable in the abstract, critics suggested that the standards of eligibility were all too often unreasonable.

In October, 1963, a Senate evaluation of the Kerr-Mills program contended that the measure was "at best an ineffective and piecemeal approach to the health problems of the Nation's 18 million older citizens." [3]

To secure whatever medical services may be provided, the applicant for MAA must shroud himself in the welfare cloak. He must present a case proving, in essence, that he cannot take care of himself. He must document the insufficiency of his resources by stating, precisely, the amount and source of his income, and the value of each asset. In many States, similar statements are demanded of his relatives. [4]

The "welfare" aspects of the Kerr-Mills MAA program, including cumbersome investigations of eligibility, plus the requirement in most States that resources of an older person must be depleted to a point of near-dependency, have further reduced participation. [5]

The critics argued that free medical care under the Kerr-Mills program had an unpleasant air of charity about it. Moreover, the eligibility requirements often required that elderly patients actually become "charity cases"—by spending all they had—before they were able to qualify for assistance.

As a result of criticism such as this, another, more sweeping

3. "Medical Assistance for the Aged: The Kerr-Mills Program, 1960–1963," a report by the Subcommittee on Health of the Elderly to the Special Committee on Aging, United States Senate (Washington: U.S. Government Printing Office, October, 1963), p. 1.
4. *Ibid.*, p. 29.
5. *Ibid.*, p. 2.

bill was introduced in 1964 and enacted by the Congress on July 30, 1965, as the "Social Security Amendments of 1965" —better known as Medicare. Financed through an increase in Social Security withholdings, the law provided medical assistance to the aged without regard for their financial status. The debate surrounding the enactment of the legislation is a matter of recent history, and was a focal point of the 1964 presidential campaign. The American Medical Association, claiming to represent 90 percent of the nation's physicians, openly and heatedly opposed passage. Still, many medical figures spoke out in support of the measure, and medical opinion, although tending heavily toward opposition, was nonetheless divided.

Faculty Members and Medicare

The present survey of medical school faculty members was conducted after the passage of the Medicare legislation but before it went into effect. Given the importance of this issue in medicine, a question was asked to assess faculty orientations.

The single most controversial social issue in medical circles this last year has been that of Medical Care for the Aged (Medicare). As you understand this program, what is your overall opinion of it?

_____ Strongly approve   _____ Disapprove somewhat

_____ Approve somewhat   _____ Strongly disapprove

The responses given by the sample of teaching physicians reflects their atypicality among American physicians. Thirty-three percent said they "strongly approved" of Medicare, while another 40 percent "approved somewhat." Only about one faculty member in four disapproved of the program. Why did faculty members approve of Medicare?

Before turning to the images of man and social moralities which constitute the focus of this book, we ought to consider the validity of another explanation implied in the criticisms of

Medicare. Throughout the testimony on this issue, the specter of an interfering government was evoked. Physicians argued that government involvement in medical care would restrict their professional services. They would be limited to those procedures which would be reimbursed by the program, unable to provide the care they felt was needed most by patients. There was talk of the government assigning patients to physicians and vice versa (despite governmental assurances to the contrary).

All in all, it was argued that government intervention in the healing process would destroy the effectiveness of day-to-day medical care. Practicing physicians contended that they knew best what had to be done in patient care, and the intrusion of a third party would hamper their efforts.

If these were the true grounds for opposition to Medicare, the overall support discovered among medical school faculty members would be understandable. When compared to private practitioners, faculty members are less intimately involved in the actual provision of medical care. Although many of them care for hundreds of patients in the university context, this is not the exclusive activity of all faculty members. Thus, it might be concluded that faculty members were more approving of Medicare than was the medical profession as a whole because they did not fully appreciate the requirements of the patient-physician relationship and could not realize the potential dangers of the government program.

Whereas the present study is limited to faculty members, it is not possible to test this hypothesis. At the same time, we may approximate a test of it by examining faculty attitudes toward Medicare in terms of faculty patient care. If medical opposition to Medicare were truly based on the professional concerns just discussed, we should expect to find greater resistance to Medicare among those faculty who are the most familiar with, and involved in, the problems of patient care.

Table 33 examines faculty service as attending physicians

in the university hospital in relation to their attitudes toward Medicare. The data in this table certainly do not support the hypothesis that opposition to Medicare represents a better understanding of patient-care problems. Neither length of service in the non-private ward service nor the number of patients attended bears any relation to the degree of approval for Medicare.

TABLE 33

ATTITUDES TOWARD MEDICARE—BY UNIVERSITY PATIENT CARE

Length of service as an attending physician for non-private patients in the university hospital	Percentage who approve of Medicare
1 or 2 months	77 (145)
3 or 4 months	79 (101)
5 or 6 months	61 (36)
7 to 11 months	77 (31)
12 months	69 (32)

Number of non-private patients attended in the university hospital	
10 or fewer	55 (9)*
11 to 25	72 (68)
26 to 40	81 (53)
41 to 60	80 (40)
61 to 80	83 (18)
81 to 100	77 (26)
More than 100	72 (90)

Note: Number in parentheses represnts number of cases on which percentage is based.
* Note the small number of cases on which percentage is based; presented for descriptive interest only.

Participation in the university ward service, however, is not the only indicator of familiarity with the problems of patient care. The primary opposition to Medicare was expressed by private practitioners. Conceivably, there is something peculiar to private practice which would be threatened by Medicare. If so, even medical faculty members deeply involved in caring for university patients would not be aware of the dangers. While most of the full-time faculty members in the present study do not engage actively in private practice, it may be noted that the majority carry on at least a limited practice of their own, and some are quite active. Table 34 presents the relationship between faculty members' private practices and their attitudes toward Medicare.

TABLE 34

ATTITUDES TOWARD MEDICARE—BY PRIVATE PRACTICE

Number of private patients per week	Percentage who approve of Medicare
None	76 (179)
Less than 5	75 (159)
6 to 10	72 (53)
11 to 25	78 (36)
More than 25	40 (20)

Note: Number in parentheses represents number of cases on which percentage is based.

Among those faculty members who report seeing more than twenty-five private patients per week, we note that support for Medicare is relatively low (40 percent approve). This discovery would tend to support the hypothesis that familiarity with patient care (private-patient care, at least) makes faculty members more sensitive to the dangers of Medicare. The hypothesis is seriously weakened, however, when the remainder of the table is examined. The greatest approval of Medicare is found among the faculty with the second largest private practices: among those who see between eleven and twenty-five private patients per week, 78 percent approve of the government program. Furthermore, private practice and Medicare are not related among those with smaller practices.

With the exception of the low approval of Medicare among those faculty members with very large private practices, there would appear to be no support for the hypothesis that approval of Medicare was based on an ignorance of its dangers.

Although participation in patient care is not related to approval of Medicare among faculty members, one might argue that *interest* in patient care is related. It might be argued that while many faculty members engage in various types of care activities, they are not particularly concerned with this aspect of medicine. We have seen that many faculty members are more interested in scientific matters than in patient care, even though they take care of patients in the university. Perhaps their greater commitment to science makes them less concerned with the potential dangers of Medicare for patient care.

This explanation is certainly weakened by the earlier findings that scientific faculty members appear as committed to the traditional norms of humane relations to patients as are the nonscientific faculty. Nevertheless, we cannot be sure that their scientific concerns would not make them less sensitive to the long-range problems of patient care. Moreover, at first glance, the data suggest that the explanation might be true.

TABLE 35

ATTITUDES TO MEDICARE—BY SCIENTIFIC ORIENTATIONS

	Index of Scientific Orientations			
	Low			High
	0	1	2	3
Percentage who approve of Medicare	58	66	77	83
	(48)	(116)	(146)	(115)

Note: Number in parentheses represents number of cases on which percentage is based.

Approval of Medicare is positively related to scientific orientations, as table 35 indicates. Among those scored lowest on the index, 58 percent approve of Medicare, and approval increases steadily across the table to 83 percent among the most scientific. Regardless of their participation in patient care (university or private), those faculty whose primary interests lie in medical science are the most likely to support government-sponsored medical care. At this point, then, one might argue that many faculty members approved of Medicare because they were not especially concerned about the dangers of government interference in patient care.

This explanation, while it makes some sense, clearly does not present the whole picture. Criticism of Medicare, and of other government-sponsored and proposed programs, has also dwelt on a moral issue which is not directly related to federal interference with the practitioner. This moral issue was voiced by the AMA when it responded to the contention that "everybody has a right to medical care."

And doesn't everybody have a right to enough to eat, to a home, to clothing, and to the other necessities of life? Where do you draw the line at how many of these things the Government should provide? Isn't it sounder philosophy to say that everybody has a right to equal opportunity to work and provide for his own needs? Which brings you back to that basic decision: are you a do-it-yourself type or a let-Sam (Uncle Sam) do-it type? [6]

The moral issue of individual responsibility was also elaborated by Dr. Bauer in his testimony before a congressional committee in 1949. "It is the belief of the medical profession generally that the primary responsibility for the health of individual citizens rests on the individual citizen and his immediate family." [7] Bauer went on to point out that if individuals could not provide for their own needs, local organizations should as-

6. This quotation is taken from the AMA publication, *The Pill That Could Change America: An Up-to-Date Review of Socialized Medicine in the World Today* (Chicago: AMA, 1959), and presented in "The Federal Government's Role" (n. 1 above), p. 13.
7. Louis Bauer, quoted in "The Federal Government's Role" (n. 1 above), p. 10.

sist. If the latter could not satisfactorily meet the needs, the state might be called upon, and only as a last resort should the federal government become involved. "We believe that this procedure is in accordance with sound American tradition, with the intent of our political principles, and with the maintenance of self-reliance and independence of each of these levels of relationship from the citizen to the National Government." [8]

One need not look very hard to find other examples of the contention that every person is responsible for providing for his own medical needs. Government assistance is seen as corrosive of that responsibility, and immoral as a result. This belief is evident in the comments of a Catholic clergyman. "Let's not rob the individual of his God-given rights to solve his own problems, to think and act for himself, to be as we all were some time back, rugged and responsible individuals." [9]

From this viewpoint, then, each individual is ultimately responsible for meeting his own needs, whether they be medical, economic, or other. Thus, some observers have suggested that shortcomings in the administration of medical care may be attributed to the breakdown of individual responsibility, to a lack of initiative on the part of the sufferer. It has been contended that where medical facilities are available and within the financial grasp of patients, patients are often too lazy to take advantage of those facilities. An AMA statement suggested that "it isn't just the financial barrier that keeps people from going to doctors—often it is just plain lethargy." [10]

The line of reasoning just considered is, of course, identical to the free-will image of man and individualistic morality dis-

---

8. *Ibid.,* p. 10.
9. Rt. Rev. Monsignor A. C. Dalton, testifying before the U.S. Senate Special Subcommittee on Problems of the Aging, October 14, 1959, reprinted in *Federalized Health Care for the Aged?* (Chicago: AMA, 1963), p. 126.
10. Quoted in "The Federal Government's Role," p. 14.

cussed earlier. It is the thesis of this chapter, moreover, that the primary basis for opposition to Medicare is to be found in precisely these concerns. Faculty members who believed that man is the master of his own fate, and thereby obligated to take care of himself, would see Medicare as a denial of that morality. Those who believed that man is largely constrained by his environment and other factors he cannot control—old people are the victims of a changing economy—would see Medicare as a realization of the new social morality.

TABLE 36

ATTITUDES TOWARD MEDICARE—BY IMAGE OF MAN

	Free-Will Image-of-Man Index						
	Low 0	1	2	3	4	5	High 6
Percentage who approve of Medicare	100	98	91	85	70	47	11
	(19)	(44)	(68)	(86)	(89)	(73)	(19)

Note: Number in parentheses represents number of cases on which percentage is based.

The free-will image-of-man index presented in table 36 includes the image-of-man-attitude items, plus the religious and political predispositions to those images. It may be noted that each component of the index is individually related to evaluations of Medicare, and the cumulative effect of these components is enormous. All of those faculty scored lowest on the index approve of Medicare; among those scored highest, only 11 percent approve.

It is now evident that faculty attitudes toward Medicare are closely related to their beliefs about the nature of man. Those who believe that each man is capable of making his own way in life oppose Medicare. Those who believe he is largely a product of his environmental circumstances support Medicare. Moreover, the relationship between images of man and Medicare is far stronger than the relationship observed with regard to the professional factors examined earlier. We may conclude, therefore, that attitudes toward Medicare are more a function of philosophical than of professional orientations.

This line of reasoning may be taken one step further. We recall that the free-will image of man is negatively related to scientific orientations among faculty members. Or, in other words, the science-oriented faculty are more deterministic in their outlooks than are the nonscientists. It is possible, then, that the earlier observed relationship between scientific orientations and attitudes toward Medicare was simply a result of different images of man. Thus, science-oriented faculty may be more approving of Medicare only because they are more deterministic, and nonscientific faculty may disapprove only because of their greater commitment to the free-will image.

Table 37 tests the hypothesis that professional orientations are related to Medicare only by virtue of differences in images of man. Faculty members have been grouped according to their images of man, and within each group, approval of Medicare has been computed for both the scientists and nonscientists. Two observations from the table confirm the hypothesis.

First, we note that the overall effect of scientific orientations on Medicare attitudes is equal to 14 percentage points—79 percent of the scientists approve, contrasted with 65 percent of the nonscientists. Yet when images of man are held constant, the effect attributable to scientific orientations is diminished in each of the partial relationships, ranging from 9 to −4 percentage points.

The second confirmation of the hypothesis is found in the last column in the table, labeled "adjusted total." In view of the difficulty of interpreting the overall effects of control vari-

TABLE 37

ATTITUDES TOWARD MEDICARE—BY IMAGES OF MAN
AND SCIENTIFIC ORIENTATIONS

Percentage who approve of Medicare	Free-Will Image-of-Man Index						
	Low 0 + 1*	2	3	4	High 5 + 6*	Total	Adjusted total§
Scientists†	100	86	87	70	44	79	75
	(48)	(51)	(54)	(44)	(43)	(240)	(240)
Nonscientists‡	92	90	78	69	36	65	70
	(12)	(20)	(27)	(39)	(47)	(145)	(145)
Percentage difference	8	−4	9	1	8	14	5

Note: Number in parentheses represents number of cases on which percentage is based.
* These scores have been combined in view of the small number of cases available for analysis.
† Defined as score of 2 or 3 on the index of scientific orientations.
‡ Defined as score of 0 or 1 on the index of scientific orientations.
§ These percentages represent the degree of approval to be expected from the scientific and nonscientific faculty if both groups were identical with regard to images of man. The standardization procedures used are those suggested by Morris Rosenberg (see text).

ables in tables such as the present one, Morris Rosenberg has suggested the use of a standardization technique similar to that used by demographers.[11] Following the logic of Rosenberg's procedure, it would be suggested that if the relationship between scientific orientations and Medicare attitudes is primarily a function of differences in images of man, then the original relationship would not have appeared if scientists and nonscientists did not differ with regard to the images of man. Thus, by statistically standardizing the images of man for both groups, it is possible to determine what their attitudes toward

11. Morris Rosenberg, "Test Factor Standardization as a Method of Interpretation," *Social Forces*, October 1962, pp. 53–61.

Medicare would have been if their images of man were empirically identical.[12]

The final column in table 37, then, presents faculty attitudes toward Medicare when images of man are standardized. If scientists and nonscientists were identical in their scores on the free-will image-of-man index, we would expect 75 percent of the former and 70 percent of the latter to approve Medicare. Thus, if the two groups did not differ in their images of man, they would not differ significantly in their attitudes toward Medicare.

The findings of table 37, therefore, disconfirm the hypothesis that scientific faculty members approved of Medicare because they didn't care about its potential dangers, being more interested in science. Interests in science, per se, have virtually no effects on attitudes toward Medicare.

The thesis advanced by this chapter is confirmed, however. Teaching physicians framed their own attitudes toward Medicare on the basis of their images of man and commitments to general social moralities. Those who were committed to the free-will image of man and the individualistic morality based upon it regarded Medicare as a threat to morality. Those holding the opposite views, however, regarded Medicare as a realization of morality.

Summary and Conclusions

This chapter has had two purposes: one specific, one general. First, we have sought to examine some of the implications of the rise of a new social morality for the future of American medicine. It was suggested at the outset that the deterministic image of man and the emphasis on equality inherent in the new social morality would encourage a new commitment to the belief in medical care as a basic human right.

12. Appendix A contains a more detailed presentation of these computations.

The empirical examination of faculty attitudes toward Medicare showed the validity of this expectation. To ensure that opposition to Medicare did not reflect a greater awareness of and concern for the problems of patient care by some faculty, we began the examination by testing this hypothesis. It was soon apparent, however, that differential experience in patient care did not affect attitudes toward Medicare. Only the index of scientific orientations was strongly related to faculty attitudes, and this was shown to reflect the differential images of man held by scientists and nonscientists.

The free-will image-of-man index provided the best explanation for approval and disapproval of Medicare. Thus, it appears that support for the program arose out of faculty commitments to the new social morality. This would indicate that the increasing acceptance of this moral position will result in new medical programs similar to Medicare, reflecting a belief that medical care is a human right rather than a commodity to be sold to those who can afford it.

The more general purpose of this chapter was to examine the nature of faculty members' formation of opinion on sociomedical issues. It was pointed out that we are now entering an era in which old traditions are being challenged, old values and norms are being reconsidered. Since medical people will have an important influence on the changes that will occur in medicine, it is important for us to understand how they will reach their decisions on the many issues.

The preceding analysis suggests a general conclusion in this regard. Faculty members' attitudes on the issue of Medicare were based, not on medical concerns, but on concerns of general social morality. This may be said of both those who supported Medicare and those who opposed it. Both groups formed their opinions on the basis of the same concerns that informed the opinions of laymen. Medical expertise did not enter in.

This conclusion is extremely important. When Medicare was being debated in Congress and across the nation, the opinions of physicians were considered particularly relevant. As those closest to the problems of patient care, physicians were invited to present expert testimony. It was implicitly assumed, therefore, that a physician's evaluation of the program would be better informed than that of a layman.[13] The findings of the present chapter show that the "expert testimony" of physicians on sociomedical issues is anything but "expert."

Chapter six pursues this general conclusion somewhat further. In a short analysis of faculty members' attitudes on the issue of infanticide, it will be apparent that medical concerns are again irrelevant. Nonmedical, social orientations are the deciding factors.

13. In all fairness to the Congress, it should be noted that they were not doggedly committed to this assumption. They did, after all, override the overwhelming objection of the medical community as a whole.

CHAPTER SIX

The Right to Die

We have already noted that the new social morality in America is likely to have important effects on the structure of medical care in the future. The renewed belief in medical care as a basic human right suggests a medical departure from the traditional structure of private practice on a fee-for-service basis. At the same time, the new social morality and the belief that medical care is a human right are not the only factors that will affect the future of American medicine.

Many other developments are having critical, far-reaching effects on the basic foundations of medicine. Consider, for example, the recent breakthrough in organ transplants. With hearts, kidneys, and other vital organs being transplanted from one person to another, countless questions are being forced upon us regarding not only medicine but life itself. With a limited number of organs available, how will recipients be chosen? When a living donor is involved (e.g., kidney transplant), what is the proper balance between danger to the donor and potential benefit to the recipient? What is the proper reaction to the person who altruistically volunteers a vital organ to save the life of one he loves or esteems? [1] These are only a few of the immediate dilemmas presented by the advent of organ transplants.

The transplantation of real organs, as well as the development of artificial ones, also raises questions as to the nature of life itself. Does human identity pose a limit on the tinkering that can be done? " 'There's nothing anyone can do,' the old man whispered. 'Even without your gadgets, medic, you know what's wrong with me. You can't mend a whole body, not with all your skills and all your fancy instruments. The body wears out. . . . And even if you gave me a new body, you still couldn't help me, because down deep, where your knives can't reach and your instruments can't measure, is the me that is old beyond repair.' " [2] If this passage from a science fiction novel sounds melodramatic, compare the comments of Michael DeBakey, a pioneer in the fields of artificial hearts and heart transplants, speaking about the artificial heart four years later: "Should this life-saving device be made available to every patient, even the hopeless victim of stroke, cancer or senility? Or, should an unbending and restrictive criterion for use be outlined? When does one determine death due to other causes? And who decides when to terminate the power flow in such cases?" [3]

How does one determine death? The very distinction between life and death is now being questioned as a result of the innovations in artificial organs and organ transplants. For centuries, this has been pretty much a closed issue. Heart stoppage has been the accepted criterion for death. Now it is insufficient: a transplanted or artificial heart may be put in its

1. Reportedly, the assassination of Senator Robert F. Kennedy produced a number of inquiries from people wishing to donate whatever vital organs might be necessary for the senator's survival.
2. James Gunn, *The Immortals* (New York: Bantam Books, 1962), p. 71.
3. Michael DeBakey, quoted in *The New York Times*, April 24, 1966.

place; lung-heart machines may keep a damaged heart beating even though the body itself has ceased to function.

This dilemma has brought forth new suggestions for the criteria of death.[4] The most common suggestion proposes the absence of brain activity in the place of the absence of heart functioning. (One reason for this suggestion is a concern for the earlier removal of organs for transplantation.) Whatever the outcome of these discussions, the simple fact of questioning and reconsideration here is the significant point. Issues which were resolved centuries ago are now being reconsidered, and the new resolutions are likely to have tremendous moral and philosophical implications.

It should be unnecessary to point out that these implications are not limited to the lives of physicians. Everyone will be affected. Nevertheless, it is probable that physicians will have a special influence in shaping the resolutions to even the most basic sociomedical issues. It is vitally important, therefore, that we understand the bases for the decisions which they are likely to reach.

The present survey did not provide sufficient information for the full examination of the several issues mentioned above. Indeed, the broad discussions of some of the issues had barely begun at the time of the survey, some four years ago. This provides an indication of the speed with which these issues are coming to a head.

One item in the 1965–66 survey of faculty members is relevant to the present discussion, however. Throughout medical history, the primary role of the physician has been to save

4. It is a commonplace to note the tremendous power of the physician in affecting the life and health of his patients. The present debate over the definition of death points to an even greater power, which physicians have exercised all along: the power to decide whether life even exists in a given case. The casual signing of a death certificate represents a professional power, the significance of which has probably not been truly appreciated until the present.

lives and to restore and protect health. At the same time, the question of when a physician might be justified in taking the life of his patient has been recurrently raised. A patient's desire to die, extreme suffering, a terminal prognosis, a dangerous pregnancy: these are some of the conditions in which it has been suggested that the physician might be justified in taking a life. In American medicine, however, the suggestions have been overwhelmingly vetoed.

A few years prior to the present survey, the medical profession was shaken by a tragedy of international proportions, which again raised the possible justification of infanticide and abortions. It was believed that this episode might provide the possibility of studying faculty attitudes regarding the taking of a life and permit an analysis of the sources of their attitudes.

A Medical Tragedy

The recent advances in pharmacology are unparalleled in the history of drug therapy. Drugs now may provide effective treatments which previously were only provided, if at all, by the surgeon's knife. At the same time, physicians have worried about their occasional inability to judge the long-run safety of many new drugs. This concern was expressed in the lead editorial of the February 18, 1961, edition of the *Lancet,* a British medical journal. The editor noted in part: "The pharmaceutical industry, conscious of what its contributions can mean, may be pardoned if it sometimes comes to think of the practitioner as an agent or distributor, whose most useful function is to apply its latest discovery." [5] Good intentions notwithstanding, the writer concluded that new methods were needed to insure the proper testing of new drugs before they were prescribed broadly by physicians.

The same issue of the *Lancet* contained a full-page adver-

5. From an editorial entitled, "Impartial Information," *Lancet,* February 18, 1961 (No. 7173), p. 379.

tisement also stressing the need for safety in drugs. A small girl was pictured in the act of taking a bottle of pills from the family medicine cabinet. The text of the advertisement read as follows: "Consider the possible outcome in a case such as this—had the bottle contained a conventional barbiturate. Year by year, the barbiturates claim a mounting toll of childhood victims. Yet it is simple enough to prescribe a sedative and hypnotic which is both highly effective . . . and outstandingly *safe*. 'Distaval' (thalidomide) has been prescribed for nearly three years in this country. . . ." [6]

Distaval, like Contergan, Asmaval, Tensival, Valgis, and Valgraine, seemed safe indeed. Laboratory experiments showed that dogs could be given one thousand times the normal dosage with no side effects. Letters to the editor of the *Lancet* during the winter of 1959 cited clinical examples of patients inadvertently taking massive overdoses with no side effects. In this regard, Distaval, like the other sedatives based on α-pthalimidoglutarimide, seemed a vast improvement over the conventional barbiturates. As it turned out, its primary shortcoming lay in the tendency to produce deformed babies.[7]

Britain and West Germany seem to have suffered most from thalidomide. From January 1, 1960, to August 31, 1962, the British estimated "there are between 200 and 250 living children with limb deformities resulting from thalidomide and a further 5 with deformities other than those of the limbs." [8] The Ministry of Health did not attempt to estimate the number of abortions undertaken to prevent deformed births.

6. An advertisement in the *Lancet,* February 18, 1961, p. 22. It should be pointed out that the *Lancet* later served as an active forum for letters and articles uncovering and documenting the dangers of thalidomide.
7. Information pertaining to the pharmocology of thalidomide is based on the Ministry of Health Reports on Public Health and Medical Subjects, No. 112, "Deformities Caused by Thalidomide" (London: Her Majesty's Stationery Office, 1964)
8. *Ibid.,* p. iii.

In September, 1960, the William S. Merrell Company sought government approval to market Kevadon (thalidomide) in the United States. Dr. Frances O. Kelsey of the Federal Drug Administration refused to approve sale of the drug until its safety had been adequately documented. Despite mounting pressure from the drug company, she was still reviewing clinical tests when the danger of thalidomide was finally uncovered.[9]

The primary issue generated by the thalidomide episode was one of drug control. Although Kevadon never received FDA approval, pills had been sent to more than a thousand physicians throughout the country. Many were given to expectant mothers. The fact that this could happen shocked the nation into a reconsideration of drug-control methods.

The administration of the pills on the eve of discovering their danger raised another issue, hotly debated in America and elsewhere. What could a woman do in the knowledge that she might give birth to a tragically deformed baby? Abortion was one solution. Unable to obtain a therapeutic abortion in Arizona, Mrs. Sherri Finkbine flew to Sweden. In so doing, she added fuel to a growing national and international controversy.

Although many people were directly affected by the thalidomide episode and were forced to make moral decisions of their own, physicians faced the greatest dilemma of all. Many bore the guilt of prescribing the pills to patients. Others were approached by anxious prospective mothers and asked to perform abortions. Every physician who delivered a deformed thalidomide baby met the moral issues of abortion and infanticide face-to-face.

The empirical examination that follows will consider the

9. Morton Mintz, *The Therapeutic Nightmare* (Boston: Houghton Mifflin Co., 1965). See chapter 12.

bases on which medical people resolved the issue of infanticide. The sample of medical school faculty members were divided in their attitudes, and we shall examine why.

Faculty Attitudes toward Infanticide

The sample of teaching physicians questioned in this survey were presented with the following hypothetical situation.

During the recent thalidomide alarm, many prospective mothers reportedly asked their physicians to allow their babies to die at birth if any bizarre deformities were present. If a physician had complied with such a request and was being tried for murder, do you think you would be sympathetic to his case or not?

_____ Definitely sympatheic   _____ Probably not sympathetic

_____ Probably sympathetic   _____ Definitely not sympathetic

Overall, the faculty respondents sympathized with the hypothetical physician. One-third said they would be "definitely sympathetic," and another one-third would be "probably sympathetic." The more important question, however, relates to why some were sympathetic while others were not.

Since the initial research concern of this book was to examine the effect of science on morality in medicine, scientific orientations among faculty members were considered a source of attitudes on this item. The common rhetoric critical of science would suggest that scientists are unconcerned with the value of human life and would, therefore, easily condone the hypothetical case of infanticide. Of course a consistent finding of this book has been the disconfirmation of such beliefs about medical science. Thus, we should be especially cautious in assuming that science would have an effect in this instance.

The data presented in table 38, however, indicate that scientific faculty members are indeed more likely to condone

TABLE 38

INFANTICIDE—BY SCIENTIFIC ORIENTATIONS

	Index of Scientific Orientations			
	Low 0	1	2	High 3
Percentage sympathetic to doctor*	54 (48)	64 (115)	74 (147)	70 (114)

Note: Number in parentheses represents number of cases on which percentage is based.

* Percentage who said they would be "definitely sympathetic" or "probably sympathetic" to the doctor who was being tried for murder as a result of complying with his patient's request to permit her deformed thalidomide baby to die.

infanticide in the terms of the hypothetical situation. Among those lowest on scientific orientations, 54 percent say they would probably or definitely be sympathetic to the hypothetical doctor. The extent of sympathy increases to 64 percent among those scored *1* on the index, to 74 percent among those scored *2,* and drops off slightly to 70 percent among the most scientific. Overall, there appears to be a positive correlation between scientific orientations and support for infanticide.

Before concluding that scientific faculty members have less respect for human life—a common allegation, which has been consistently refuted in the preceding analyses—we should consider some alternative explanations. Since the issue under consideration is a moral issue, it will be wise to examine the influence of the new and old social moralities which were the subject of examination in chapters three through five.

The traditional, individualistic morality was based, we recall, on a belief in the individual human being as inherently sacred. Each individual was viewed as the possessor of free will and was accountable for his actions. He was held personally responsible for his economic, political, and moral behavior. One might suppose, then, that the individualistic morality would provide a strong barrier to the physician's taking of an individual life—even the life of a badly deformed, newborn baby.

The new social morality, on the other hand, is based on a belief that the individual is severely limited in his possibilities for action by factors he cannot control. From this perspective, a deformed baby would be seen as facing nearly insurmountable odds. Surely, the new social morality would support social programs for providing welfare benefits to such people; but it is also possible that faculty members informed by this morality might be the more likely to condone what they believed to be a humane and merciful act: letting the baby perish immediately rather than having to face a life of suffering.

TABLE 39

INFANTICIDE—BY FREE-WILL IMAGE-OF-MAN INDEX

	Free-Will Image-of-Man Index						
	Low 0	1	2	3	4	5	High 6
Percentage sympathetic to doctor	89	89	75	74	62	51	44
	(19)	(44)	(68)	(86)	(89)	(72)	(18)

Note: Number in parentheses represents number of cases on which percentage is based.

Table 39 supports these expectations. Sympathy for the hypothetical doctor is highest among those who are uncommitted to the traditional morality: 89 percent of those scored 0 or 1 on the index say they would at least probably be sympathetic. At the other extreme, only 44 percent of those most committed to the traditional morality would be sympathetic.

Additional data suggest that the relationship between scientific orientations and support for infanticide may be explained away in terms of social morality. Table 40 presents the joint effects of science and morality on responses to the hypothetical case of infanticide. When scores on the free-will image-of-man index are taken into account, the effect of scientific orientations becomes very ambiguous. Among those committed to the new social morality (scored *0–2* on the index), the relationship between science and sympathy for the doctor is negative—the opposite of the original relationship. Among those scored as medium or high in their commitments to the traditional morality, there is no consistent relationship. Within each group on the index of scientific orientations, the original relationship between morality and sympathy for the doctor is retained—with the single exception of those scored *0* (the least scientific).

TABLE 40

INFANTICIDE—BY SCIENTIFIC ORIENTATIONS AND
FREE-WILL IMAGE-OF-MAN INDEX

	Percentage sympathetic to doctor			
	Index of Scientific Orientations			
Free-Will Image-of-Man Index	Low 0	1	2	High 3
Low: *0–2*	* (7)	92 (25)	85 (52)	73 (41)
Medium: *3–4*	45 (20)	76 (45)	72 (61)	74 (38)
High: *5–6*	62 (13)	38 (34)	57 (23)	58 (19)

Note: Number in parentheses represents number of cases on which percentage is based.
* Too few cases for a stable percentage.

The findings of table 40 may be added to a series of earlier findings which pointed to the irrelevance of science on specific issues of medical morality. Scientific orientations, in and of themselves, do not affect (*a*) compassion, (*b*) responsibility, (*c*) concern for experimental subjects, (*d*) support for Medicare, or (*e*) support for infanticide. Those who believe the observed rise of science in medicine will upset or distort medical morality ought to reconsider. Although scientific innovations surely create moral dilemmas which need to be resolved, scientific orientations per se do not undermine traditional moral positions.

Tables 39 and 40 suggest that the new social morality provides an encouragement for the acceptance of infanticide in certain situations. When the data are examined more carefully, however, this conclusion is found to be somewhat misleading. Among the several components of the free-will image-of-man index, only religion is significantly related to sympathy for the doctor.

Among Roman Catholic faculty members, only one-third say they would be sympathetic to the hypothetical doctor. Sixty-nine percent of the Protestants and 84 percent of the Jews expressed sympathy. The agnostic faculty were less sympathetic (78 percent) than the Jews, but more sympathetic than either the Protestants or Catholics. When religiosity is added to religious affiliation, the effect of the religious factor is even clearer, as table 41 shows.

These findings will surely come as no surprise to many readers. During the thalidomide episode, the religious factor was clearly in evidence. A papal communication to Mrs. Finkbine pointed out that abortion was considered as evil as murder among Catholics. And the Roman Catholic position on infanticide is equally unequivocal. The doctor who permitted even a deformed baby to die, even at the mother's request, would face the charge of having committed a mortal sin. An orthodox Catholic would be hard pressed indeed to be sympathetic. Table 41 reflects these factors. Roman Catholic faculty members, in general, are the least sympathetic to the

TABLE 41

INFANTICIDE—BY RELIGIOUS AFFILIATION AND RELIGIOSITY

	Percentage sympathetic to the doctor			
Religious affiliation	Question: How important is your religion to you?			
	Extremely important	Fairly important	Fairly un-important	Not at all important
Catholic	24 (33)	38 (26)	46 (13)	* (4)
Protestant	50 (38)	71 (83)	73 (71)	84 (19)
Jew	* (6)	79 (29)	86 (35)	94 (16)

Note: Number in parentheses represents number of cases on which percentage is based.
* Too few cases in these cells for stable percentages.

hypothetical doctor, and their sympathy decreases with in-creasing religiosity.

Protestant and Jewish opinions on the thalidomide issue were more equivocal. Some clergymen defended the use of therapeutic abortions, while others opposed such acts. It is understandable, therefore, that Protestant and Jewish faculty members would be more sympathetic than were their Catholic colleagues. Even among Protestant and Jewish faculty, how-ever, we note that sympathy decreases with increasing religios-ity. Religious faculty in general, then, object to infanticide more than do the irreligious. Infanticide is a broad religious issue rather than the special concern of only one religious denomination.

We shall not pursue the examination of religious differences any further in this context. Surely much more could be said to explain the reason why Jewish faculty members, for example, are more permissive than are the Protestants, but this is not the primary concern of the present study. For our purposes, the simple fact that infanticide is seen and resolved as a religious issue among medical school faculty members is the point of the examination.

The thalidomide tragedy provided a new stimulus for debates over the morality of abortions, infanticide, and euthanasia more generally. Many of these debates have taken place among physicians who believe they are discussing a question of medical morality. In the sense that the debates concern a question of morality within a medical context, we may conclude that medical morality is involved. But if one assumes that peculiarly medical norms and values lie at the base of the debate, one is sorely misled.

When physicians debate the morality of infanticide, they do not speak as medical men, their opinions are not informed by peculiarly medical concerns. Rather, they speak as Catholics, Protestants, Jews, and agnostics. They speak as religious men and as irreligious men. In short, their opinions are based on the same (religious) factors as those which inform the opinions of laymen. A very religious Catholic physician and a very religious Catholic plumber are both likely to oppose infanticide as immoral. The source of their opposition is to be found in their shared religious perspective, however, not in medicine or in plumbing.

This was the same as the conclusion reached in the preceding examination of Medicare. Although physicians were given special attention during the consideration of the national legislation, it is now apparent that the medical testimony offered before Congress did not reflect medical concerns at all; it reflected only philosophical positions, which were represented among laymen as well as among physicians.

When we consider the wide range of moral issues which the medical community will attempt to resolve in the years to come, we see that it will be vitally important that we understand the sources of attitudes and opinions. Despite their medical context, these issues represent general concerns of social morality; physicians will resolve them on the basis of general concerns rather than on the basis of medical expertise. We might ask, therefore, whether physicians should make such decisions at all.

This book began with an interest in determining the effects of scientific orientations on medical morality. It has moved from that initial concern to much broader issues of social morality. We have seen that the important question is not limited to the influence of science on medical morality, but is concerned rather with the influence of social morality on all of medicine. Chapter seven will review the major substantive findings of the preceding analyses and will attempt to place them in their proper perspective.

CHAPTER SEVEN

Summary
and Conclusions

As promised at the outset, this book has wandered considerably from the initial research concerns which stimulated the survey of medical school faculty members during the 1965–66 academic year. It has moved from a limited concern for the impact of science on humane patient care to a much more general examination of medical and social morality. It will be useful at this point to review the primary substantive findings of the book and retrace the connecting theme of the analyses. Having done this, we shall turn to a reconsideration of those findings as they relate to medicine, to medical education, and to the study of other professions as well.

REVIEW OF FINDINGS

Measuring Scientific Orientations

Whereas the study began with a concern for the impact of scientific orientations among medical school faculty members, chapter one addressed the problem of distinguishing the scientific from the nonscientific faculty among the sample responding to the survey. Three items in the questionnaire appeared to reflect faculty subjective inclinations to scientific concerns: (*a*) their ultimate interests in problems of understanding basic mechanisms rather than total patient management, (*b*) their greater interest in literature dealing with the basic rationale underlying new therapeutic treatments rather than the effectiveness of those treatments, and (*c*) their self-identification as researchers rather than as practicing physicians. Faculty responses to each of these items were highly intercorrelated, and a composite index of orientations was constructed from them.

The index was first validated on the basis of its power to predict faculty responses to other items which also measured subjective orientations to science. Next, the index was examined in relation to faculty members' actual participation in research activities. Although the index was intended to measure *subjective* orientations to science, it was discovered that such orientations were also highly related to participation in science. Those designated as "scientists" in the subsequent analyses, then, are both subjectively and objectively more scientific than the remainder of their colleagues.[1]

Finally, the index of scientific orientations was examined with regard to age, academic rank, and era of medical training in an attempt to determine the presence of a trend toward science among medical school faculty. One may tentatively conclude that such a trend does exist, although the data provide only an approximate test; furthermore, the data suggest that the trend may be more complex than is imagined.

1. That the index is intended to provide a *relative* measure of scientific orientations bears repeating. There is no pretension that those faculty designated as "scientists" in this study are really scientists in any ultimate or absolute sense. They are only more scientific than those who received lower scores on the index. Wherever the language of the text suggests more than this, it only results from an attempt to ease the presentation of data and ideas.

The Effects of Science on Care

The frequent allegation that scientific medicine undermines the traditional norms of humane patient care was tested in chapter two. The present study provides data relating to three norms: compassion, responsibility, and concern for experimental subjects.

First, faculty members were presented with a hypothetical situation in which one of their university hospital patients had died. They were then asked whether they would personally speak to the members of the surviving family or if they would delegate this task to the house staff. It was felt that speaking to the family personally would represent a greater degree of compassion. Scientific and nonscientific faculty members did not differ in their responses to the question. It was tentatively concluded, therefore, that science does not undermine compassion in patient care.

Second, two items in the questionnaire dealt with the manner in which faculty members arranged for the care of their patients in the university hospital. The first was based on a recognition of the necessity for faculty members to rely on the house staff for much of the day-to-day care of their patients: they were asked how they arranged for the house staff to report to them on patient care. Those who required the house staff to report daily at a specified time were considered to be more responsible in caring for their patients than were those who did not require house-staff reporting except "when it was necessary."

The second item reflecting faculty-member responsibility for their hospital patients asked them to report the procedures by which major diagnostic and therapeutic decisions regarding their patients were made during those hours when the faculty member was off duty. Those who said they were personally called to make such decisions were considered more responsible than those who reported that either house staff members or on-duty faculty members made such decisions.

Again, it was found that scientific and nonscientific faculty members did not differ. The index of scientific orientations was not related to faculty responses to either of the questions. Science, therefore, did not appear to undermine responsibility for patients.

Finally, faculty members were asked whether they believed a medical researcher was obligated to participate as an experimental subject in any experiments which would endanger the health or lives of his subjects. Support for his participation was taken as an indication of a faculty member's concern for the human worth of experimental subjects. It is frequently alleged that scientific physicians are less sensitive to this concern, viewing subjects only as guinea pigs, but the data in this instance again pointed to no difference between scientists and nonscientists.

In view of the consistency of the findings in chapter two, it was concluded that science does not undermine the traditional norms of humane patient-physician relations. If medical morality is being threatened, it is necessary to look elsewhere than to science for the threat.

The Bases of Scientific Morality

Despite the consistent findings of chapter two, it must be conceded that science and morality have conflicted throughout history. Thus, although science does not present a direct threat to the traditional norms of humane patient-physician relations, it is still possible that medical science and morality conflict in other ways.

The introduction to part two advanced the thesis that the traditional morality of American medicine, and of American society in general, was based on a free-will image of man. Each individual was conceived of as the master of his fate, personally bearing the responsibility for his own successes or failure in life. It was suggested, however, that this traditional image of man is being progressively replaced by another, more deterministic image of man. This latter image of man places a greater emphasis on the environmental and other factors which limit man's freedom and help determine his life situation.

The deterministic image of man has arisen largely out of the social sciences; but it was suggested that since science, generally, involves a deterministic component, even medical scientists might be more likely to accept determinism in human affairs as well as in biological issues. The conclusion to be drawn, then, was that the rise of science in medicine coincides with the spread of the deterministic image of man and the new social morality based upon it.

This thesis was tested through an examination of the relationships between scientific orientations and commitments to the value systems traditionally associated with the free-will image of man. Overall, religion and science were found to be incompatible. Moreover, Catholicism and Protestantism—hypothesized as the most involved in the free-will image—produced fewer scientific orientations than did Judaism or agnosticism. Finally, conservative politics—a bastion of the free-will image—was also found to be incompatible with science.

The analysis then turned to a consideration of two attitudinal items designed to provide a more direct measure of the two images of man and the social moralities based on them. As expected, religion, politics, and science were all related to these additional items. The thesis was again confirmed.

The examination of images of man and the new and traditional social moralities provided an insight into the relationship between science and morality in contemporary medicine. Although science was not found to directly threaten the traditional norms of humane patient-physician relations, it is apparent that science is part of a much broader movement, which will greatly undermine the basic moral foundations of both American medicine and American society.

Science, Morality, and Patient Care

In view of these findings, it was necessary to examine the possible consequences of the new social morality on the traditional norms of humane patient-physician relations. In chapter four, the analysis focused on the joint effects of science and morality on the measures of compassion, responsibility, and concern for experimental subjects. Overall, it was discovered that neither science nor the new social morality represents a threat to the traditional norms, even though they both threaten to undermine more general moral positions.

It was concluded that the new social morality offers a new moral basis for humane relations among men. In place of the more traditional emphasis on individual responsibility, the new social morality stresses the responsibility of society for the failures and sufferings of its members. This orientation is combined with a greater valuation of equality, suggesting more programs of social welfare throughout society.

The Right to Medical Care

Perhaps the most evident effect of the new social morality in medicine concerns the view of medical care as a basic human right. In place of the traditional fee-for-service system of remuneration—based on a belief in the responsibility of the individual to provide for himself—the new social morality calls for the provision of medical care to all in need. In the case of those who cannot afford to pay for the necessary care, it is the responsibility of the society to make payment for them.

The empirical analysis in chapter five examined faculty members' attitudes toward Medicare. Whereas many critics of the program argued that it would interfere with the practice of medicine, we turned first to indicators of faculty members' participation in patient care for the source of their attitudes. One possible explanation for their differences might have lain in their differential knowledge of practical medicine. Ultimately, however, medical differences were judged irrelevant to attitudes on this issue.

As was suspected, faculty members' images of man provide the only answer to differences in attitudes toward Medicare. Those who believed man to be a free-will agent—personally responsible for making his own way in the world—opposed the program as immoral. Those who believed that man's successes and failures are largely determined by forces he cannot control supported the program as being especially moral.

This examination provided an insight into the future effects of the new social morality in medicine. At the same time, however, it raised an even more basic issue. Medical school faculty members, in framing their opinions on a seemingly medical issue, were more informed by social than by medical factors.

The Right to Die

Chapter six pursued the general issue somewhat further. The new social morality only represents one, albeit important, reorientation of American values in response to radical changes in society and to technological advances. It was pointed out that a wide range of basic moral and philosophical positions are now being questioned and new positions are being taken. Since physicians will be especially influential in establishing the new philosophical and moral positions regarding issues in the medical context, it is particularly important to discover how their opinions will be formed.

The present study provides data on faculty responses to a hypothetical situation of infanticide. This is one of the many basic issues being reevaluated in the medical profession today. It was discovered, however, that medical concerns are again irrelevant to faculty opinions. In this instance, their religious orientations appeared to be the most salient determinants. Like their attitudes on Medicare, their attitudes on infanticide reflect social rather than medical concerns.

This concludes the review of major findings from the preceding analyses. Now we shall turn to a discussion of what they mean for more general issues in medicine and in the sociological study of professions.

THE OVERLY PROFESSIONALIZED VIEW OF MEDICINE

Socialization is a favorite concept for sociologists. And well it might be, for it is a keystone in any perpetuated social structure. By the same token, the professionalization process has been given a central place in the sociological analysis of the professions. The primary concern of many studies has been, How do neophyte professionals come to accept the norms and values traditionally associated with their professions?

It is worth noting that the two best-known studies in medical sociology were addressed to precisely this topic. Merton and his colleagues took a rather conventional approach to professionalization.[2] Having elaborated the norms constituting the medical role, the investigators set about determining how different aspects of medical school training led students to accept those norms. The off-beat and irreverent tack taken by Becker and his colleagues, on the other hand, was more open-ended.[3] They asked simply, What effect does medical school have on students' images and orientations toward their chosen profession? Both studies, however, were addressed chiefly to the professionalization process among medical students, assuming that medical school training either directly (Merton) or inadvertently (Becker) shaped students' futures as physicians.

2. Robert K. Merton et al., *The Student-Physician* (Cambridge Mass.: Harvard University Press, 1957).
3. Howard Becker et al., *Boys in White* (Chicago: University of Chicago Press, 1961).

Unfortunately, the present study has not provided information pertaining to the student experiences of the sample of
faculty members. Yet the information which has been available
for examination suggests, indirectly at least, that sociologists
may have overemphasized the effects of medical training.

Regarding a variety of medical issues, we have found faculty
members' overall social and philosophical perspectives to be
far more influential than strictly professional experiences or
orientations. Therefore, even if the character of medical school
training has an influence on the types of medical careers chosen
and pursued by physicians, these effects may still be irrelevant
to the quality of patient care they provide or to their attitudes
on issues such as Medicare and infanticide.

These findings are admittedly indirect and tentative, but
they must be added to a growing literature supporting the same
conclusions. Research by Fred Davis and Virginia Olesen,
for example, indicates that the professionalization process
among nursing students is far less clear-cut than was formerly
imagined.[4] Jerome Carlin reaches a similar conclusion with
regard to lawyers and legal ethics.[5]

I do not suggest, nor do the authors just cited, that profes-

4. See, for example, Fred Davis and Virginia L. Olesen, "Baccalaureate
Students' Images of Nursing: A Study of Change, Consensus, and Con-
sonance in the First Year," *Nursing Research* (Winter 1964), and Virginia L. Olesen and Fred Davis, "Baccalaureate Students' Images of Nursing: A Follow-up Report," *Nursing Research* (Spring 1966). Dr. Davis
approaches the topic even more directly in "Professional Socialization as
Subjective Experience: The Case of Student Nurses," mimeo, presented
to the International Sociological Association, September 1966, in Evian,
France.

5. Jerome Carlin, *Lawyers' Ethics* (New York: Russell Sage Foundation,
1966). Carlin finds legal ethics most closely related to lawyers' socio-
economic status (SES) backgrounds and the character of their current
practices. Lawyers from high SES families and those practicing in prestigious firms are the most faithful to established legal ethics. The relationship between legal ethics and law school training seems primarily a
function of these other two variables. High SES students tend to attend
high quality law schools, and graduates of those law schools have a better chance of joining prestigious firms. On balance, however, the independent effect of law school on ethics appears minimal.

sional training has no influence on the nontechnical orientations of professionals toward their trades. The professionalization process is real and important. Nevertheless, the present
study, among many, points to the danger of overemphasizing
this one source of professional orientations at the expense of
other sources which, in some instances, wholly eclipse the current influence of professional training per se. To put it bluntly,
some "medical" orientations are largely predetermined before
students arrive at medical school, and no amount of medical
training will change them.

This contention is worth overstating, since it is so easily
ignored by sociologists and medical educators alike. But to
appreciate fully the importance of this point, we must go even
further to recognize that some of the nonmedical sources of
medical orientations have their impact very early in life. One
example should suffice.

In the examination of attitudes toward Medicare, we recall
that faculty members' images of man appeared to be the most
important single determinant. While not mentioned at that
time, we may now note that geographical region also influenced faculty attitudes. Those who report growing up in the
East were relatively more supportive of Medicare (84 percent
approved) than those raised elsewhere. Those raised in the
South were the least supportive (49 percent). The effect of
regional origins on attitudes toward Medicare, then, represents
35 percentage points. These data, however, are based on where
faculty members grew up.

When the region of medical training is examined, those
trained in the East are still the most supportive of Medicare,
and those trained in the South are the least supportive, but the
regional effect in this instance only represents 25 percentage
points. A closer examination, moreover, indicates that this
latest finding only reflects the greater likelihood that faculty
attended medical school in the same region in which they were

raised. As table 42 shows, the region of medical training has virtually no effect on Medicare attitudes when regional origins are controlled.

TABLE 42

MEDICARE—BY REGION OF UPBRINGING AND REGION OF
MEDICAL TRAINING (EAST AND SOUTH ONLY)

	Percentage who approve of Medicare	
Region of medical training	Region of upbringing	
	East	South
East	84	50
	(159)	(38)
South	80	47
	(20)	(34)

Note: Number in parentheses represents number of cases on which percentage is based.

Regardless of where they attended medical school, faculty members raised in the East are much more likely to support Medicare than those raised in the South. Yet when region of upbringing is held constant, those trained in the East are only slightly more supportive of Medicare than those trained in the South, the difference being so small as to be insignificant. Thus, to the extent that region affects attitudes toward this sociomedical issue, the regional influence occurs at an early age. In this sense, the die had already been cast by the time our respondents arrived at medical school.

There are two primary implications of these conclusions as regards the operation of medical schools. First, we must realize that medical educators do not possess as much power for shaping the future of medicine as many people have believed. Far more attention must be paid to the orientations and perspectives which medical students bring to medical school originally. While the structure and character of formal medical school training is undoubtedly important, its impact can only be understood in the context of initial student perspectives. As Samuel Bloom has concluded: "The most important conclusion to this analysis is that student and physician attitudes toward the patient as a dehumanized, segmentalized, institutionalized entity are *not* conceived as the direct result of a given kind of environment which is interpreted as the single primary cause of the attitude. Instead, the prior expectations which students bring with them to the preclinical years are shown as selective determinants which contribute to attitudinal learning." [6]

As a result, we must recognize that innovations in medical school curricula can have only partial effects on the ultimate medical orientations of the students being trained. And even if family-practice courses and apprenticeship programs succeed in persuading more students to enter general practice, for example, there is no guarantee that humane medicine will be enhanced thereby. In all likelihood, some of the additional general practitioners would be compassionate and responsible, while others would not. We simply cannot escape the conclusion that good people make good doctors, and a person's "goodness" is largely determined prior to his entering medical school.

This conclusion is no doubt an unsatisfactory one for most medical educators, yet it is not unique to this study. This is not the first time that sociological research has produced findings which suggest that conditions cannot be changed very much directly. As only one example, Jacob Feldman conducted a study of health information among the American people.[7] His goal was to discover the sources of high levels of

6. Samuel W. Bloom, "Some Implications of Studies in the Professionalization of the Physician," *Patients, Physicians and Illness,* ed. E. Gartly Jaco (Glencoe, Ill.: Free Press, 1958), p. 319.
7. Jacob J. Feldman, *The Dissemination of Health Information* (Chicago: Aldine Publishing Company, 1966).

health information so that public health officials might disseminate information more effectively in the future. His most salient finding: better educated people are better informed about health. Therefore, the best way to increase the level of health information in the country would be to upgrade education.

In the case of medical education, however, the picture is not quite so gloomy. To produce better physicians, it is not necessary that all Americans become more compassionate and responsible. Instead, more enlightened recruiting of medical students would surely help. It is by now well known that white, upper-middle-class males are grossly overrepresented among medical students. Yet none of these characteristics is necessarily related to the humane qualities most desired in physicians. If medical school recruitment were more attuned to the qualities of compassion and responsibility and if the existing sex, race, and financial barriers were finally destroyed, the quality of American medicine might be immeasurably improved.

The first general implication of our findings, then, is that medical schools do not possess as much power for shaping medical orientations as has been supposed. The second general implication is related to the first. If the four years of medical school are to have any effect on nontechnical orientations, a direct rather than an indirect approach seems to hold the greatest potential. For lest I seem overly deterministic, let me state the belief that medical students can be changed over the course of four years. But those changes can only be brought about, I suggest, by conscious and direct efforts.

If important medical perspectives are based on more general social and philosophical orientations rather than on professional experiences, it stands to reason that changing the nature of professional experiences will not affect the general perspectives. Thus, assigning medical students to assist general practitioners in the community probably will not make them more compassionate. Studying the question of compassion itself in detail might have some influence, however. Rather than hope that medical students will develop the "right" attitudes by being placed in the "right" situations, it would make more sense to discuss the "right" attitudes directly, in relation to specific medical contexts.[8]

This more direct approach to general medical perspectives might be most effective in those instances where the social determinants of medical attitudes can be documented. Thus, for example, if students can be persuaded that attitudes toward Medicare are based on philosophical images of man rather than on medical experiences, they might be able to examine more fruitfully their basic philosophical perspectives per se. Since attitudes toward infanticide are based on religious considerations rather than medical ones, this issue should be discussed openly as a religious issue, not disguised as a medical one.

I would hope that the findings of this present analysis would provide materials with which to begin more reasonable discussions among medical students and faculty. At the same time, much more information is needed ultimately.

THE NEED FOR FUTURE RESEARCH

The conclusion that professionalization is often overemphasized by sociologists and medical educators is only partially useful. If commitments to humane medical care are rooted in general social perspectives, this only tells us where to look for answers, not the answers themselves. The present study has suggested the beginnings of this enterprise but has left more

8. This is the intention of Guttentag's proposed course entitled "The Medical Attitude," and it seems a wise one. Otto E. Guttentag, "A Course Entitled 'The Medical Attitude': An Orientation in the Foundations of Medical Thought," *Journal of Medical Education*, October 1960, pp. 903–907.

questions unresolved than it has resolved. The continuation of the search must have two foci.

First, it is still necessary to refine the concepts relating to humane medicine. I have attempted to utilize the best materials available in the present study. Nevertheless, the theoretical constructs used here and their empirical referents must be judged relatively crude, and a good deal more work is necessary.[9] Hopefully, however, this examination has demonstrated the necessity for distinguishing the quality of patient care from simple participation in it. It is grossly inaccurate to assume that scientific concerns are an alternative to human concerns or that medical scientists are necessarily less humane as physicians.

The second task facing researchers in this area, of course, concerns the search for the sources of those social perspectives which reinforce the human aspect of medicine among physicians. The present analysis has barely scratched the surface in this regard, and the task is surely a formidable one. Given the present selectivity of medical school recruitment, it is conceivable that studies of medical students and of physicians will not permit the discovery of all the most important social sources. It would seem wiser, therefore, to conceptualize the relevant social perspectives in the most general terms and then

9. Dr. Alan Barbour at the Stanford Medical School and Dr. Windsor Cutting at the Hawaii Medical School have independently suggested that the item used to measure compassion in this study is somewhat ambiguous. When faculty members were asked whether they would personally speak to the family of a deceased patient or whether they would delegate this task to the house staff, it has been assumed that delegating the duty was an indication of less compassion. As both of these medical educators have suggested, it seems likely that many faculty members would delegate the duty as part of their obligation to train the house staff to perform such services. In the present report, I have attempted to accommodate this possible ambiguity by combining the first two responses offered as my measure of compassion. Clearly, future researchers should be especially careful to take into account the teaching obligations of faculty members.

seek their sources in society at large. To cite one example, the study of images of man might be more wisely conducted on a broad social scale rather than just among medical personnel. Discoveries relating to the general social sources of these perspectives would point to the implications of present medical-school recruiting policies and would suggest ways for improving the quality of medicine.

THE CONTROL OF AMERICAN MEDICINE

The findings just reviewed have another implication, which has been mentioned previously but which deserves emphasis. The close intertwining of social and medical perspectives raises a very important question regarding the control of medical care in America.

Traditionally, the professions (and occupations generally) have been granted special powers of advice and control. Certain professions have been permitted to set their own standards of training and ability and to police the performance of their members. And when legislative action has been required in a specialized area, specialists from that area have been asked to advise on the best measures to be taken. For the most part, this procedure seems quite rational. The cancer researcher is surely better qualified to advise on the allocation of cancer research funds than is the plumber or the sociologist.

At the same time, such expert advice has been regarded more warily in some instances. Particularly, we are wary of the vested interests which may bias the expert testimony of specialists. Thus, for example, when the major automobile manufacturers testified before Congress regarding the need for additional auto safety equipment, few people believed that corporate self-interests were irrelevant to the testimony offered. By the same token, the opponents of Medicare were sometimes criticized as fearing they would make less money under the proposed program. (Of course, some proponents of Medicare were accused of hoping to make more money.)

The findings of this study have shown that expert testimony may be biased in more subtle ways as well. Faculty members' attitudes toward Medicare and infanticide were based on nonmedical philosophical and religious perspectives which they themselves may not have realized as such. Thus while some opponents of Medicare, for example, could say quite genuinely that they were not looking out for their own interests, their testimony might have been discredited as being "nonexpert" even when it was not motivated by self-interest.

I suspect that future research will indicate that many other attitudes on nontechnical medical issues depend on social rather than medical perspectives. What is called for, then, is a more careful evaluation of the situations in which professional experience is truly the key determinant of professional pronouncements, and when the answer is to be found in nonprofessional perspectives.

IMPLICATIONS FOR THE STUDY OF PROFESSIONS

This report has focused almost exclusively on a single profession. Indeed, most of the empirical data presented are taken from one small segment of even that profession. Nevertheless, I believe the findings of this single study can at least suggest fruitful lines of research in other professions and in the study of professions in general.

The contemporary conflict and concern regarding medical science and traditional care of patients may be viewed in a much broader context. The rise of science is part of a more general development occurring within medicine and indeed within most professions. Traditionally, the professions have been organized around the application of special expertise in the service of clients. Physicians (teachers, ministers) provide patients (students, parishioners) with the benefit of their medical (academic, religious) training. And sociologists have devoted considerable attention to the normative structures which regulate the professional-client relationships through which services are provided. Yet increasingly, the professions include roles which do not involve the direct provision of services to clients. Today we find "doctors" without patients, "teachers" without students, "ministers" without parishioners.

The appearance of these nonservice professional roles— often involving administration of services, teaching others to serve, or basic research—have frequently produced crises in normative regulation. The traditional norms governing the application of professional expertise in relationships with clients are often irrelevant (or even dysfunctional) when applied to professional activities which are devoid of clients. To some extent, of course, new norms have been established to regulate the new roles. Thus, to some extent, the medical researcher is excused from certain traditional ethics of healing, and in turn is bound by norms derived from the procedure of the scientific method. Frequently, however, the distinctions between various professional roles are vague, and many professionals find themselves cross-pressured by both service and nonservice norms.

This is the situation examined in this report. We have been interested to test the allegation that professionals who are chiefly oriented to nonservice functions (e.g., research) may perform the traditional service functions badly. Many of the general criticisms directed at nonservice physicians are also echoed in other professional contexts. Perhaps the best-known instance of this concerns the debate over teaching and research among university faculties in general.

The great similarity between the medical situation discussed above and the criticisms to be heard on other university campuses immediately suggests that some empirical verification is in order. Are research and teaching mutually exclusive? Does the growth of academic research in and of itself reduce the quality of university instruction? I suspect research similar to that which was presented in this report might point to some revisions in the current polemical arguments. At the very least, our medical experience should point to the need for empirically verifying such common beliefs.

More generally, however, the basic distinction between service and nonservice professional roles requires additional refinement and analysis. Certainly, the lesson of the recent past is that nonservice professional roles are increasing in numbers and proportions. At the same time, bureaucratic and technological developments have reduced the manual tasks and the client contacts required even of professionals in the service of clients. As mentioned earlier in this report, professionals are often cast in the role of service managers today. Developments such as these are clearly leading us away from more traditional patterns of professional care.

Many people see in these changes a threat to the human aspect of professional service. Moreover, we have seen the pragmatic and moral concerns, which support the need for maintaining that human aspect in medicine, and similar arguments could no doubt be made in other professional contexts as well. This writer is personally committed to the belief that the human aspect must be maintained in medicine and elsewhere. But the implications of this study suggest that the simple reaction against change is not the answer. What is required is a more careful articulation of the desired humanitarian foundations of future social relations, and then a hardheaded attempt to accomplish them.

Afterword

My interest was most whetted by the new perspective *Science and Morality in Medicine* brings to old but still salient questions about free will and determinism; it is on this theme that I shall concentrate my remarks.

The questions of whether or not man is possessed of free will and what would be implied for moral responsibility were it to be established that he is not, while the subject of extensive philosophic and scientific inquiry, remain unresolved. By now, informed opinion is probably dominated by the belief that these questions are beyond man's capacity to decide. Yet, the debate continues.

Most past and present discussion about free will and determinism has been highly abstract. Logic and reason have been the primary tools of discourse. Evidence, if any, has been drawn almost exclusively from the natural sciences. And the thrust of virtually all inquiry has been to establish whether free will exists or not; not how much freedom of choice there may be.

Largely ignored in classic treatment is that, whatever the

facts may be, man nevertheless makes assumptions about the existence of free will and how it operates, and that these assumptions do have consequences for moral judgment, moral responsibility, and, more generally, for the quality of social life. A singular contribution of Prof. Babbie's book is to make this truth manifest and to demonstrate its operation empirically.

There is a potential in such empirical research for altering the course of traditional inquiry into free will and determinism. What assumptions man does make, and what moral consequences they have ought to be, it would seem, grist for the mill of such inquiry.

However, it is not primarily philosophers whom I intend to address but social scientists. It is they, I would suggest, who stand to benefit most from the new perspective which this book brings to these age-old questions. Professor Babbie himself has demonstrated the power of his conceptualization of images of man to illuminate understanding of how attitudes are formed on contemporary moral issues. To his discussion I would add the following remarks to hint at still broader implications.

How much man is in command of his destiny and how much he is the victim of uncontrollable forces beyond himself are matters about which men in every age have made assumptions. And, throughout recorded history, there has never been a time in which the common assumption was that man's life was wholly determined for him, although societies have differed radically in their estimates of how much free will a man does possess.

Particularly in the West, the nature of the external forces operating on man has been understood as divine. But divinity has not always been central, or even present, in deterministic philosophies. The forces to which man is subject have also been conceived as inviolate principles or laws of creation.

Such conceptions, found more frequently in the East, are illustrated by the ancient Chinese belief in a natural harmony of order in the universe and in Hindu ideas of *nirvana* and the law of *karma*. In addition, there have been conceptions which deny the supernatural but nevertheless postulate forces transcendent of man and capable of exercising authority over him. The economic determinism of Marxism is such a force as are the eternal regularities asserted by modern science.

All of these conceptions impose certain conditions and limitations on the human experience. Some things are fated for man and beyond his capacity to change; that he live his life as an outcast, for example, if the operation of the law of karma has brought him to that lowly birth; or, that he accept fatalistically what life brings because it has so been willed by Allah.

However, within the framework of these eternal verities, some room is always left for man to decide for himself. Thus, even in Islam where it is accepted that man's very being and existence have been foreordained, there is still an injunction to do Allah's will and therefore an assumption that man is free to elect to do so or not.

Taken together, prevailing assumptions about how much free will man possesses (images of man) and about the forces to which man is subject (images of "god") have always been important elements in the organization of social life. The ideological warrant for closed societies of the past and present—feudalism in medieval Europe, caste in ancient India, oligarchy in modern Communist states—has come primarily from prevailing images of "god" and man. That class lines are not so tightly drawn in the West may not be directly attributable to the prevailing imagery, but it is nevertheless consistent with it. In America and Western Europe, the effect of what amounts to a radical free-will image of man is exhibited not only in a relatively open class structure but also in systems of law and of social welfare and in political, religious, and economic institutions grounded in the belief that man is in control of his own destiny and therefore, justifiably held accountable and responsible for the choices he makes.

But images of man and of "god" do not remain static, and when they change it can be expected that there will be changes in the organization of social life as well. Professor Babbie illustrates this very ably in his adroit analysis of the shift in America from a radical free-will image of man to a more deterministic one. While the shift is still in process and the old image still retains power, the effects of the new image are already being felt. No longer is it taken for granted that the poor are poor because they fail to exercise their free will in a responsible fashion. No longer is it assumed automatically that the murderer deserves to be punished because he had the choice and therefore the responsibility for his act. No longer are the problems of Negroes and other minority groups ignored because they are thought to be the individual's own fault. The shift from traditional morality to a new social morality may not be wholly accounted for by a changing imagery of man; but as Professor Babbie shows, prevailing images of man—and, I would add, of "god"—are in the process of change, and the change parallels, supports, and abets, if it does not cause, the changing social morality. As regards the American image of "god," it is increasingly what modern science—the natural, and increasingly the social sciences—tells us about the forces beyond man's control which are coming to count, as God, traditionally conceived, loses his power to inform.

Professor Babbie's empirical work does not constitute a test of all of his theoretical ideas about images of man and their effects. He is able to demonstrate convincingly, however, that it does matter for moral judgments what image about free will is harbored. It turns out that those most disposed to a deterministic image of man are more prone than those committed to a free-will image to exhibit moral compassion in their interpersonal relationships and in their attitudes towards social issues in which understanding of the nature of man is central.

This hardly decides the classic question, of course, since it is clear that the determinist posture of the physicians studied is relative, rather than absolute as in the classic formulation. Still—and here I return to the philosophical implications of Professor Babbie's findings—it would appear of some importance to the quality of social life that the new image of man is increasingly a deterministic one, albeit so far on the soft side. Should the image turn hard and the dominant view become that man is almost wholly determined, the moral implications might not be so benign. And yet, it may well be that contemporary science is destined to lead us to that harder image.

It is still an open question how much illumination can be brought to our understanding of social structure, social change, and the quality of social life, by examining more systematically how such phenomena are related to ideas about man's degree of free will and the forces which limit it. Professor Babbie's observations and empirical research do not establish, of course, what the potential might be. They do suggest, as these remarks have sought to testify, that a more extended effort to find out would seem worth the substantial sociological investment it would take, and would have an additional payoff for philosophical speculation about the good life.

CHARLES Y. GLOCK
Department of Sociology
University of California at Berkeley

Appendixes

Methodological Notes

This appendix is designed to present a variety of issues which were not wholly appropriate for presentation in the main body of the text. It begins with a discussion of some general methodological conventions employed in the analyses. Then we shall consider some more specific points, organized here according to the chapters they refer to.

General Comments

Most of the analyses contained in this report have been limited to a cross-tabulation format, as it seems more appropriate to the research goals and the nature of the data being examined. Two general percentaging conventions have been employed which ought to be made clear. First, in virtually all cases, percentages have been computed on the basis of those faculty members who gave relevant responses to the questions. Nonrespondents, then, have normally been omitted as irrelevant to the table presentations. In each instance, the number of cases upon which the percentages are based have been indicated either beside the notation "100 percent =" or, in more complex tables, in parentheses below the percentages they refer to.

Second, all percentages have been rounded off to the nearest whole percent. Carrying out percentage computations to several decimal points seems to indicate a degree of precision which does not pertain in most surveys, and I have not wished to give the impression of such precision in this case. Hanan Selvin is reputed to have said that all survey percentage computations should be rounded off to the nearest *even* percent, reasoning that any survey finding whose significance is affected by a difference of one or two percentage points shouldn't be taken too seriously in the first place. While I have not been quite this radical in the preceding analyses, I have been guided by essentially the same reasoning.

Several composite indexes have been used in the preceding analyses to measure general variables among faculty members. Some readers may have preferred the use of more rigorous scaling techniques in the place of simple indexing. Primarily, I have chosen to construct indexes because of a personal disinclination to change responses or to answer questions which faculty members themselves chose to skip over. Thus, indexes have been constructed, and scores have been assigned only to those faculty members who answered all the questions upon which the indexes were based.

The methodological notes below pertaining to chapter one examine the issue of indexing versus scaling somewhat more closely. In particular, it is noted that the key index in the study —that of scientific orientations—is essentially a scale despite its construction as an index. Changing faculty members' answers to create a scale in this instance would have had little effect on the scores assigned to each.

These are some of the more general conventions followed in the report. The remainder of this section is devoted to a chapter-by-chapter consideration of more specific points. In some instances, I simply elaborate on the more technical aspects of various procedures, while in others I pursue some of the methodological avenues which were not sufficiently developed for a lengthy discussion in the text.

Chapter One—The Index of Scientific Orientations

The reader will recall that faculty members' scientific orientations were measured in this study through the construction of an index which combined responses to three questions as follows.

Score

1. As a medical school faculty member, in what capacity do you feel you can make your greatest *teaching* contribution: as a practicing physician or as a medical researcher?

Practicing physician 0
Medical researcher 1

2. As you continue to advance your own medical knowledge, would you say your ultimate medical interests lie primarily in the direction of total patient management, or the understanding of basic mechanisms?

Total patient management 0
Basic mechanisms 1

3. In the field of therapeutic research, are you generally more interested in articles reporting evaluations of the effectiveness of various treatments or articles exploring the basic rationale underlying the treatments?

Primarily articles evaluating effectiveness 0
Both types, but somewhat more interested in articles evaluating effectiveness 0
Both types, but somewhat more interested in articles exploring basic rationale 1
Primarily articles exploring basic rationale 1

Some readers may object that an ordinal scale would have been more appropriate in this regard. Indeed, the three items used in the index are clearly scalable, and I considered this procedure at one point. Ultimately, however, I decided to work with the simple index because of my reluctance to tinker with faculty responses so as to permit scaling. This decision was further supported by the observation that 90 percent of the simple index scores represent ideal scale types without any modification. This may be seen in table A-1.

TABLE A-1

THE SCALABILITY OF SCIENTIFIC-ORIENTATION
INDEX SCORES

	Item 1[a]	Item 2[b]	Item 3[c]	Number of Cases
Scale Types	+	+	+	116
	+	+	−	127
	+	−	−	92
	−	−	−	48
			Total	383
Mixed Types	−	+	−	18
	+	−	+	14
	−	−	+	5
	−	+	+	7
			Total	44

Note: Science-oriented responses are designated with a plus (+). Non-science-oriented responses are designated with a minus (−).

[a] "In the field of therapeutic research, are you generally more interested in articles reporting evaluations of the effectiveness of various treatments or articles exploring the basic rationale underlying the treatments?"

[b] "As you continue to advance your own medical knowledge, would you say your ultimate medical interests lie primarily in the direction of total patient management, or the understanding of basic mechanisms?"

[c] "As a medical school faculty member, in what capacity do you feel you can make your greatest *teaching* contribution: as a practicing physician or as a medical researcher?"

Thus, while simple index construction was used in this instance, the reader should realize that it essentially produces a scale nonetheless.

Chapter Two—Medical Science and Patient Care

The analysis of scientific orientations and faculty members' responsibility for patients was, of necessity, limited to those faculty members who reported serving as attending physicians in their university hospitals during the 1964–65 academic year. This limitation would not seem to affect the findings presented in the analysis, however, as scientific orientations are unrelated to such participation. (See table A-2.)

TABLE A-2

PARTICIPATION AS ATTENDING PHYSICIAN IN
THE UNIVERSITY HOSPITAL—BY
SCIENTIFIC ORIENTATIONS

| | Index of Scientific Orientations | | | | |
| | Low | | | High | |
	0	1	2	3	Total
Percentage who served during the 1964–65 academic year	68	82	81	73	78
	(47)	(114)	(146)	(116)	(449)
Number of months as attending physician*					
1 or 2 months	47%	48%	36%	41%	42%
3 or 4 months	28	24	27	18	29
5 or more months	25	28	37	41	29
100% =	(32)	(93)	(118)	(85)	(347)
Number of patients served*					
25 or fewer	22%	34%	20%	26%	26%
26 to 60	44	26	29	29	30
61 to 100	4	11	17	17	14
More than 100	30	29	34	28	30
100% =	(32)	(93)	(118)	(85)	(347)

Note: Number in parentheses represents number of cases on which percentage is based.

* Limited to those faculty members who report serving as attending physicians in the university hospitals during the 1964–65 academic year.

While the measures of commitment to humane patient-physician relations available to this analysis are far from perfect, there are good reasons for believing that the items examined are sufficient for this initial investigation. First, each of the items—speaking to the surviving family, supervising the house staff, and making decisions about patients—was designed to reflect examples which may be found in medical literature regarding the norms of humane care. Second, as

TABLE A-3

THE INTERRELATION OF "COMPASSION"
AND "RESPONSIBILITY" ITEMS

Percentage who would make all major decisions			
"Would you personally speak to the surviving family or delegate the duty to the house staff?"			
Almost always speak	Speak as a general rule	Delegate as a general rule	Almost always delegate
56	49	38	17
(39)	(51)	(172)	(30)
"How did the house staff report on your patients?"			
Formally every day	Informally about every day	Three times a week	Whenever circumstances required
44	43	31	24
(141)	(54)	(36)	(17)

House staff reporting	Speak to surviving family or delegate to house staff	
	Speak	Delegate
About every day	54	39
	(61)	(134)
Less often	40	27
	(20)	(33)

Note: Number in parentheses represents number of cases on which percentage is based.

table A-3 shows, the three items are empirically related to one another, further supporting the contention that all three reflect the same dimension.

Chapter Seven—Standardizing Images-of-Man Scores

To demonstrate that the relationship between scientific orientations and attitudes toward Medicare was simply a function of images of man, Morris Rosenberg's standardization procedure was used. This procedure is based on the following logic. (1) The free-will image of man is largely incompatible with support for Medicare. (2) The free-will image of man is also largely incompatible with research orientations. (3) Therefore, researchers favored Medicare only because they were inclined toward the deterministic rather than free-will image of man.

The hypothesis to be derived from this reasoning is that if scientific and nonscientific faculty members did not differ with regard to images of man, they would not differ in their attitudes toward Medicare either. To test this hypothesis, we may statistically adjust the images of man among the two groups so that they are the same. In making this adjustment, the standard chosen was the distribution of scores found among both groups when considered as a whole. (See table A-4.)

Section I of table A-4 is taken from table 37 in the main body of this report. The first line of section II presents the total number of cases for each score on the free-will image-of-man index when scientific and nonscientific faculty are combined. The second line of section II shows the proportional distribution of the 385 cases among the index scores. This is the standardized distribution of scores to be assigned to both the scientific and nonscientific faculty groups.

Following the logic of the standardization procedure, the next step would involve the redistribution of scientific and nonscientific faculty. Thus 16 percent of the 240 scientists and of

TABLE A-4

STANDARDIZING IMAGES OF MAN

	Free-Will Image-of-Man Index					
	Low				High	
						To-
	$0+1$	2	3	4	$5+6$	tal
I.						
Scientists						
Percentage favoring Medicare	100	86	87	70	44	79
Number of cases	48	51	54	44	43	240
Nonscientists						
Percentage favoring Medicare	92	90	78	69	36	65
Number of cases	12	20	27	39	47	145
II.						
Total number of cases	60	71	81	83	90	385
Proportional distribution	.16	.18	.21	.22	.23	1.00
III.						
Adjusted percentages						
Scientists	16.0	15.5	18.3	15.4	10.1	75
Nonscientists	14.7	15.3	16.4	15.2	8.3	70

the 145 nonscientists, respectively, would be assigned to the cells representing the lowest category on the free-will index. Eighteen percent of the scientists and of the nonscientists would be assigned to the cells representing scores of *1* on the index, and so forth. Once this standardized redistribution of cases had been accomplished, the percentages approving of Medicare in each cell could be multiplied by the new cell frequency to determine the (fictitious) number of approvals. Approvals among the scientists and among the nonscientists would each be totaled and divided by the total frequency in each group to produce the standardized percentage of approval.

Fortunately, a closer examination of this procedure indicates that it is unnecessary to compute the standardized distribution of cases for each group. Considering the computation for one group, if P represents the percent approving Medicare, in a given cell, F represents the total number of cases, and D represents the standardized proportional distribution of cases, then the formula for computing the standardized percentage is as follows (subscripts represent the five index categories):

$$\frac{P_1FD_1 + P_2FD_2 + P_3FD_3 + P_4FD_4 + P_5FD_5}{F} \text{ or } \sum_1^5 \frac{P_iFD_i}{F}$$

The denominator of this formula is, of course, the total number of cases in the whole group. However, we note by inspection that this same factor may be taken out of the numerator, leaving $P_1D_1 + P_2D_2 + \ldots P_5D_5$ or $\sum_1^5 P_iD_i$. In short, it is possible to simply multiply the proportional distribution pertaining to a cell by the original percentage approving in that cell; the resultant partial percentages are then simply totalled for the group.

This concludes the technical notes pertaining to the analyses in this report. Appendix B is devoted to an informal biography of the project's design and analysis. Despite the informality of the presentation, I feel strongly that the issues to be discussed are as importantly *methodological* as any of the preceding notes and computations.

Biography of Project S2205

It has been my experience that most methodology textbooks tend to present social research in such a way as to make it appear relatively straightforward, if not downright simple. Anyone who has personally conducted this type of research can, of course, verify the inaccuracy of such impressions. Nevertheless, social researchers themselves inadvertently contribute to the myth by favoring their reports in such ways as to assure readers they have been faithful to the "scientific" procedures outlined in methods texts.

There are two serious dysfunctions deriving from this tradition, I believe. First, as Phillip Hammond has pointed out, the intellectual biography of an idea is critical to our understanding of the idea itself. Such "biographical" information contributes importantly to our understanding of the scientific enterprise as such, especially regarding the relationship between theory and research. There is, nonetheless, a dearth of such information. "For very few social scientific reports, it appears, with all their discussions of methods, contain accounts of the 'method' by which they came about. There are almost no chronicles of social research. And yet this missing component is an important one, as seen in the frequency with which existing chronicles are cited as well as by the number of times eminent and experienced researchers have called for more such accounts." [1]

The second dysfunction is essentially a didactic one. All too often, neophyte researchers plunge headlong into the murky waters of empirical research, protected only by their favorite methods text. Most research administrators can recount numerous academic drownings in this sense, and most researchers can probably confess to harrowing experiences closer to home. The failure to accurately and honestly chronicle research projects as they happened is unfair to future researchers and contributes to the needless waste of substantial research funds.

The present project biography represents neither the conviction nor the hope that this project will become a model for social research of the future. Quite the contrary is my intention. Everything I have done right could no doubt be done better, but everything I have done wrong should be avoided like the plague. While I have perhaps not always risen above the temptation to rationalize the more questionable procedures, it has been my intention to tell the story as honestly as possible.

Project Design

I know relatively little about the earliest beginnings of this study since I was not present at its birth. As mentioned in the preface to this report, Professor Otto E. Guttentag of the San Francisco Medical Center instigated the survey. As a professor of medical philosophy, he had been concerned for years with what I have called the "human aspect" of medicine. Like many others in his profession, he was alarmed at the possibility of

1. Phillip E. Hammond, ed., *Sociologists at Work* (New York: Basic Books, 1964), p. 2.

today's medical students becoming technical experts at the cost of missing the humanitarian base of the healing art. For decades, Professor Guttentag wrote articles and lectured on this topic in the hope of stimulating a renewed concern within the medical profession.

Sometime in 1963, a colleague to whom he addressed such concepts suggested that he consider a survey of medical school faculty members in order to assess the current situation and to gain insights into what might be done. The same colleague gave Professor Guttentag the name of the Berkeley Survey Research Center and its then director, Professor Charles Y. Glock. As a result of this suggestion, the initial contacts were made, and a research proposal was drafted for submission to the National Institute of Health. The proposal pointed to the necessity for understanding the effects of research on the human aspects of medicine and called for a national survey of medical school faculty members in the clinical departments of Medicine and Pediatrics. The proposal was approved, and SRC Project S2205 began.[2]

Under the supervision of Dr. Glock, Dr. Robert E. Mitchell and Mrs. Elizabeth Hutmann, both of the Survey Research Center, worked with Dr. Guttentag in drafting questionnaires which would elicit the desired information from faculty members. During the first year of the project, questionnaires were circulated among faculty members at three medical colleges. The distribution and collection of questionnaires was handled by the Association of American Medical Colleges, which had agreed to permit the study to be conducted partially under its auspices.

Beginning with the summer of 1964, Dr. Mitchell and Mrs. Hutmann were no longer available. As a new research assistant at the Center, I was asked to assist Professor Guttentag in

2. S2205 was the SRC job number assigned. Such symbols take on a special meaning after years of being identified with them.

completing the project. The summer and fall of 1964 were spent in discussions with Dr. Guttentag regarding his research interests and in a concentrated reading program in medicine and medical sociology.

Before long, we had decided that the previous, piecemeal collection of data was not sufficient to our needs. Although the AAMC had been gracious enough in contacting one or two schools at a time, the selection of schools was based on participation in the AAMC continuing-education program, and the process was taking too long. What we needed was a substantial cross section of medical school faculty members across the country who could all be questioned at about the same time. Rather than work through the AAMC, then, we decided to undertake the data collection on our own.

Data Collection Phase

During the latter half of 1964, the discussions regarding the aims of the project had led to some radical changes in the content and format of the questionnaire. As a result, the questionnaires collected during the first year were of only minimal value in determining the utility of particular questions and data collection techniques. It was necessary, therefore, to conduct a pilot study with the new instrument prior to making a major commitment in the field.[3] For the purpose of this pilot study, a mimeographed questionnaire was used. (I subsequently discovered that photo-offset questionnaires would have been less expensive as well as better looking.)

The decision had been made early in the project to limit its scope to faculty members in Medicine and Pediatrics at the member colleges of the AAMC. With this in mind, the pilot-study sample was drawn from the list of those colleges, strati-

3. I am now convinced that pilot tests of questionnaires are indeed necessities rather than luxuries, and a major failure of formal methodology instruction is the failure to make this point explicit enough.

fied in the manner described in appendix C. Six schools were considered sufficient for the pilot study.

Recognizing that medical school faculty members receive questionnaires almost every day, we felt it was necessary to find some special means of encouraging participation. Conducting the study under AAMC auspices had served that purpose during the initial data collection, but that possibility had been dispensed with in the decision to move more rapidly. We decided, therefore, to communicate with the deans of each selected college and seek their support for the study.

Letters introducing the study were sent to the deans of the six medical schools selected for the pilot study. The general aims of the study were outlined, a copy of the questionnaire was included, and deans were asked for their blessings, plus a list of the full-time and part-time faculty members in their departments of Medicine and Pediatrics. In due course each replied, one or two skeptical about the value of the study, and the mailing list of faculty members was prepared.

One of the six deans, however, pointed out that since his college offered only a two-year medical course and, hence, did not offer an M.D. degree, perhaps his faculty would not be appropriate to our research goals. This had not occurred to us until then, but we quickly agreed with his point. As a result, the pilot study was conducted among the five remaining schools, and the final study design was revised to include only those AAMC members offering a regular four-year curriculum.

On March 3, 1965, mimeographed questionnaires were sent to 778 faculty members in five of the nation's medical colleges. Twelve days later, ten were returned completed. We were, of course, excited by this auspicious beginning, and our spirits remained high until the next day when only one questionnaire arrived. The return rate then proceeded to rise again until the two hundred mark was passed on April 23. On the following day a letter was sent to all faculty members in the sample. Since the questionnaires were anonymous, we had no idea who had returned them and who had not. Thus, the follow-up letter generally thanked those who might already have participated in the study and gave a generalized nudge to those who had not. This additional effort ultimately brought in only about fifty more completed questionnaires.

Now a one-third return rate on a mail questionnaire is not one of the high standards held up by methodology texts, nor is it especially cherished by researchers in the field. Nevertheless, the pilot-study questionnaires that were returned provided the information needed to examine the usefulness of the questions being considered. The next three months were devoted to this task.[4]

Finally, on August 13, 1965, a draft of the final questionnaire was sent to the university printer for production. It should be noted that this step was preceded by many hours of consultation with the printing office, selecting type formats, agreeing on production schedules, estimating costs, and designing a two-part back cover which could fold out into a gummed self-mailer to reduce the effort of returning the questionnaire. Such details may seem trivial to the nonresearcher, but their

4. The question of how one evaluates the usefulness of questionnaire items tested in a pilot study is another question that has not been adequately discussed by researchers. Certainly the overall distribution of answers to a question is one guide; the study of social variables presupposes that some variation will appear in the answers given to questions. (At the same time, however, it may be very important descriptively to know that all the respondents agree on certain points.) The relationship among responses to different questions is another guide. Certainly if responses to several items do not exhibit the empirical associations theoretically expected, something must be wrong with some of those questions (or with the theoretical expectations).

In this particular case, the questions were evaluated in several different manners, varying in explicitness. Ultimately, however, a 250-page manuscript was prepared from the analysis of the pilot-test responses, as a first draft of what the final report might look like. More than anything else, the utility of questions in meeting the analytical needs of that draft determined which items needed revision, which were missing altogether, and which could be dispensed with.

implications for the goal of obtaining valid overall information make them critical.

Next a sample of fourteen medical colleges was selected for the final survey—in the manner and for the reasons described in appendix C. A few additional comments are in order regarding the sample design chosen. In the best of all worlds, the most appropriate sample design would have been one in which a large number of colleges were selected (proportionate to their sizes) and a sample of faculty members selected from each. This design would have provided the best chance of achieving representativeness with a relatively small number of faculty members overall. Our experiences during the pilot study, however, had convinced us that medical school deans were not all that friendly to a survey of their faculty members. It seemed unlikely, therefore, that we would be successful in persuading, say, twenty-five or thirty deans to cooperate. Instead, we decided to select fewer colleges, concentrate on winning the approval of each dean, and then send questionnaires to all the appropriate faculty members at each of the schools. Lest this be passed over as a relatively simple matter, it might be instructive to report some of the project notes recorded in that process.

August 16: Letters sent to the 14 medical school deans, introducing the project and requesting permission to survey their faculties.

August 23: School A replied, approving the study.

August 30: Schools B and C approved the study; School D refused.

August 31: Selected School D' as replacement and wrote to dean.

September 13: School E approved the study.

September 20: School F approved the study.

September 21: Sent follow-up letters to nonresponding deans.

October 7: Called nonresponding deans; assured that answers would follow.

October 12: Schools G and H refused.

October 13: Selected Schools G' and H' as replacements and wrote to deans.

October 14: School I approved study.

October 15: Called School E requesting faculty list not yet received.

October 20: School J refused; selected School J' as replacement and wrote to dean. Wrote to School I requesting faculty list.

October 22: School K refused; selected School K' as replacement and wrote to dean.

October 27: School H' approved the study.

November 2: School D' refused.

November 8: Received faculty list from School E.

November 19: School G' approved the study.

November 24: School K' approved the study.

The purpose of the preceding abbreviated chronicle is not one of complaining or pleading. The deans who refused to approve the study certainly had that right, and those who delayed in making decisions are undoubtedly very busy people. I offer this only to warn other researchers against blithely saying as we did: "First, we'll write to the deans and get their blessing." It took more than three months and numerous letters and long-distance telephone calls to obtain twelve approvals (including replacements) from an initial list of fourteen schools.

Of course, a good deal more was going on during those three months. Printer's proofs of the questionnaire arrived on August 30 to be checked and revised. As faculty lists were received, the names were punched on IBM cards to permit computer-printing of address labels. In view of the rather tight budget, most of this work was done personally by the research assistant assigned to the project.

Early in the project, we had decided to maintain the anonymity of respondents to the survey. There were no funds to permit the gathering of additional information based on knowing a respondent's identity, and moreover, we felt the response rate would be higher with an anonymous format. At the same time, we anticipated the necessity of following up on those faculty members who did not reply to the first appeal. However, the pilot-study experience had taught us that a general letter sent to all those originally selected did not have much effect.

As a result of these conflicting conditions and requirements, each faculty member was sent, with his questionnaire, a postcard addressed to us and bearing a duplicate of his mailing label. He was asked to return the postcard at the same time the completed questionnaire was returned. As postcards were returned to the project office, faculty members' IBM cards were removed from the mailing file.[5] Several weeks after a wave of questionnaires had been sent, all those IBM cards remaining in the file were used to produce a new batch of address labels, and new questionnaires (and another postcard) were sent out with a letter stressing the importance of participating. This follow-up procedure was carried out twice.

After the final questionnaire wave had been mailed, we were still unhappy with the overall return rate. The budget would not stand another mailing, and furthermore, even the follow-up mailings which had gone out had not brought in many additional responses. It was at this point that we hit upon the idea of mailing to a subsample of nonrespondents a short, demographic postcard questionnaire in order to compare them with the respondents. Since address-label postcards had been sent with the third questionnaire, it would be possible to learn the names of the "hard-core" nonrespondents, thus permitting the much shorter (and cheaper) final follow-up.

5. In the beginning of the data-collection phase, we had been somewhat apprehensive about the success of the postcard technique. Clearly, any faculty member who resented our bothering him could simply toss the postcard in the mail and be done with us. This did not happen, however. For although we were not able to match postcards with completed questionnaires, the latter outnumbered the former throughout the study. At the very least, more faculty neglected to return the postcards when their questionnaires were completed than returned the postcards only.

Appendix C presents additional details on this final measure. Certainly it was one of the more rewarding afterthoughts in the project. A surprisingly high proportion of nonrespondents were willing to spend the 10–20 seconds required to check off answers to six short questions and drop the card in the mail. As a result, it was possible to test some of the response biases which might have been present. Most gratifying, of course, was the discovery that respondents and nonrespondents were remarkably similar.

Since appendix C deals with the return rates among full-time and part-time faculty, I shall not go into that aspect of the data collection here. And since the data-processing prior to analysis was relatively straightforward, this too will be omitted.

Analysis and Reporting

Textbooks tend to suggest that social research is conducted in the following manner. The researcher ponders a number of theoretical issues, forms scientific concepts, combines them into hypotheses, operationalizes the concepts and hypotheses, and finally conducts an empirical study to test those hypotheses. This did not happen in the study of the medical faculty. Some of the more interesting theoretical concepts and conclusions did not reveal themselves until I was drafting the final report on the project. Often, when faced with the task of communicating one or several findings in readable English, a conceptual link or theoretical implication seemed to jump out from the page, marking me the fool for not having seen it earlier.

More broadly, the entire analysis and reporting of the project occurred in much the same fashion. In addition to my own drafts, colleagues at the Center and the Sociology Department, books and articles in medical sociology and other fields, chance remarks in corridors, almost every conceivable stimulus could set the orientation of the analysis off on a new and more exciting tangent. Looking at this final draft, I am truly amazed that it has come so nearly full circle in returning to the basic concerns that motivated its beginning. Despite this basic return to (or persistence of) old concerns, it may be interesting to review some of the major influences which appeared during the analysis.

To the extent that I had begun with hypotheses, they probably consisted of the following. Medical school faculty members are oriented either toward patient care or toward research (the terms "healers" and "scientists" were used in one draft). To my mind, the two seemed pretty much mutually exclusive; scientists didn't think much of patient care, and healers didn't think much of science. My own bias was in favor of the scientists. Despite Dr. Guttentag's frequent remarks about the necessity of considering faculty members who were oriented to both, I managed somehow to maintain this overly simplified image.

At the same time, I had a hypothesis about the sources of scientific interests among faculty members. Professors Rankin and Glock and I had just completed a modest study on images of man and attitudes toward de facto segregation in Berkeley. I had never given images of man much thought prior to that study, and the concepts still fascinated me. There seemed no doubt that the free-will image precluded scientific pursuits, and the subsequent analysis (chapter three) seems to have confirmed that belief.

There were certainly many other issues which interested me as well as the others on the project, but I, at least, had not thought them out in any great detail. So fascinated was I with the image-of-man idea that the initial analysis conducted on the first 200 pilot-study responses involved the construction of a rough orientation index to be run against the religious and political sources of the free-will image.

It was during the glorious days of exhibiting these first findings that Dr. Gertrude Selznick forced me to reconceptualize the initial faculty-orientation index. Due no doubt to my rather crude view of science versus healing, the first measure of professional orientations included two of the items used in the present draft, plus the item "There is a tendency these days for medical research to wander too far away from actual problems of preventing and curing disease." In the beginning, this statement seemed an integral part of the patient-care position that was defended by many in the medical literature. But it was Dr. Selznick who forced me to consider the presence of an additional variable, which I began calling "antiscientism." Scientists were certainly not antiscientific in this sense, but neither were *all* nonscientists.

The interim result of this suggestion was a revision of the basic orientation index to its present constitution and one of the many attempts to create a more elaborate typology of orientations. In this latter regard, care-oriented faculty members were additionally scored as either "antiscientific" or "nonantiscientific" while the research-oriented were scored as "aware" or "unaware" in terms of their sensitivity to problems of research ethics. The typology itself proved unmanageable in analysis, however, and was not sufficiently thought out, I suspect. Nevertheless, its lengthy consideration, involving literally hundreds of computer-produced tables and probably a hundred pages of working draft, brought home the necessity of keeping the orientation index "clean." It also destroyed my implicit bias in favor of scientists as a whole. I began to consider "good guys" and "bad guys" in both camps.

The next major influence appeared in a series of tables run fairly early in the analysis. Following the construction and validation of the orientation index, I had planned a chapter entitled "The Cognitive Implications of Roles." I had intended to run the orientation index against various university activities to show that research-oriented faculty engaged mostly in research, while care-oriented faculty engaged mostly in patient care. Thus I could state that either faculty members sought out duties commensurate with their professional interests, or conversely, their actual duties had "cognitive implications" for their ultimate medical interests. These two themes are discussed in chapter two of this report, but of course the data did not wholly bear out my expectations. The research-oriented faculty cared for as many patients as did the care-oriented, and they seemed to do just as conscientious a job of it.

Probably Rodney Stark was the biggest help in steering me through this hiatus. I had begun to sense the implications of these findings for the conception of professional orientations, but talking to him about the tables and discussing our own reflections on the teaching/research distinction in university life helped develop the idea. Both of us had generally discarded the view that university researchers don't or can't teach, and Rod recalled seeing some empirical findings which indicated that the best-liked teachers, by and large, were the most prominent research scholars as well. These discussions were particularly influential in pointing to the more general implications of my findings with relation to the study of professions at large. At the same time, I finally understood what Dr. Guttentag had been saying with regard to faculty members being oriented to both care and research.

Chapter two of this report introduces the concepts of tough- and tender-mindedness and tough- and tender-heartedness. These cognitive and affective dimensions are, for me, the most exciting ones in the report, although they are about the least well developed. These concepts have a relatively long history in the project. They first came to mind as I was grappling with the professional typology mentioned above. I couldn't shake the belief that the good guys and bad guys had to be identified, but I couldn't manage to set out the guidelines for describing them.

If anything, the formulation described in chapter two was stimulated by a personal concern with politics. Grappling with the development of my own political convictions, I was at once dismayed by the often cruel and insensitive predilections of the radical left and the political naïveté of the well-meaning but ineffectual moderate left. It finally struck me that the former were often no more compassionate and libertarian than the fascists, while the latter tended to avoid facing what were sometimes unpleasant facts. Head and heart clearly had to be distinguished. This seemed as true in medicine as in politics.

This conceptualization won immediate recognition and support from everyone I discussed it with, but neither Glock, Selznick, Stark, nor I could come up with a proper conceptualization. Guttentag felt that it held the answer to his persistent warnings against oversimplification, but even so we could not adequately put it to work in the medical study. After months of feverish table-running, the enterprise had not succeeded, and the concepts began fading from the analytical scene. Not until the preparation of the final draft did these notions reappear, this time as an explanation for the commitment to the human aspect of medicine. Even so, the concepts have not been adequately elaborated, and I doubt that the medical-study data are sufficient for the task.

It will have become evident to the reader by now that this study did not follow the ideal research pattern discussed in most methods texts. Specifically, it did not issue from a general, deductive theoretical proposition and focus on the operationalization and testing of that theory. Indeed, the empirical analyses were largely divorced from any explicit theory, although countless implicit fragments of theories were involved. One draft of the report, however, did have a fairly explicit theoretical framework, and its history (and demise) ought to be instructive.

During the spring of 1967, I had occasion to take a graduate seminar from Professor Neil Smelser, examining the theories of Talcott Parsons. Students in the seminar were asked to prepare papers critically evaluating some aspect of Parsons' works. My decision to focus on his medical sociology was really a second or third choice, and one which was basically irrelevant to my work on the medical faculty survey.

The more I read of Parsons' medical sociology, however, the more I began to try applying it to the polemical literature I had been reading in connection with the survey. Parsons had characterized the medical profession in terms of his pattern variable schema: as achieved (vs. ascribed), as universalistic (vs. particularistic), as functionally specific (vs. functionally diffuse), as affectively-neutral (vs. affective) and as collectivity-oriented (vs. self-oriented). In reviewing the current criticisms of the medical profession, it seemed reasonable to expect that doctors would be criticized for violating the norms associated with the medical role. For example, one would expect to find doctors criticized for being particularistic rather than universalistic, for being affective rather than affectively-neutral, and so forth. Many of the more salient criticisms I had been reading in connection with the survey, however, pointed in precisely the opposite direction.

The primary criticism of doctors that interested me was the allegation that they were too detached and impersonal (affectively-neutral) rather than too involved with their patients (affective). Similarly, medicine as a profession has been roundly criticized for becoming too specialized (functionally specific) in comparison with the comprehensive treatment provided by the general practitioner of old (functionally diffuse). Although I realized that these applications of Parsons' concepts were not altogether faithful to his schema, the gross contradictions separating what seemed to exist and what might have been predicted were puzzling.

Late one night, after days of toying and tinkering with the pattern variable schema, the obvious chose to reveal itself to me: the pattern variables were *variables*. If their variability could be used to grossly differentiate general social roles and institutions, why couldn't a more refined use of them characterize variations within a more homogeneous group? If physicians were more universalistic than Jewish mothers, medical scientists could still be more universalistic than practicing physicians.

As I began to reconceptualize Parsons' pattern variables for the seminar paper, their relevance to the medical survey became ever clearer. Universalism-particularism, within the medical profession generally, was reconceptualized as a difference of concerns between the acquisition of generalized knowledge on the one hand, and the provision of medical care on behalf of particular patients on the other. Within the profession, specificity-diffuseness could be represented by views of the patient/subject as either an integrated, whole system (diffuseness) or as a collection of parts, each of which could be studied or treated separately (specificity).

Combining these two reconceptualized dimensions created a fourfold typology of medical orientations which appeared to represent the major orientations to be found in medicine today. Among the particularistic group (concerned with healing), those oriented to the patient as an integrated whole would be represented by general practitioners; those with a functionally specific view of the patient would be represented by specialized practitioners. Among the universalistic group (concerned with generalized knowledge), basic scientists would represent those with the functionally specific view. The final type resolved a conceptual issue which had plagued the survey throughout its history. The modern proponents of social medicine and comprehensive-care programs could be characterized as having a concern for knowledge rather than healing, and also a concern for viewing the patient as an integrated whole rather than as a collection of parts.

If universalism-particularism and specificity-diffuseness could be used to describe the major medical types, the remaining pattern variables (with the exception of achievement-ascription) seemed relevant to the remaining concerns of the analysis. Affective-neutrality approximated the objective detachment which scientific physicians were accused of carrying over into their care of patients. Reconceptualized this way, it might be used as a dependent variable for analysis within the basic framework described above.

Within the medical profession, it made less sense to me to contrast self- and collectivity-orientations than to attempt a differentiation of the collectivities to which physicians might be oriented. For the practicing physician in the traditional healing situation, the collectivity seemed to include the physician and his patient, as Parsons had suggested. For the pure scientist, however, the relevant collectivity seemed to be the community of scholars. Commitment to the patient-collectivity, then, would represent the exercise of fiduciary responsibility on the patient's behalf, while commitment to the scholar-collectivity—when it appeared in the context of patient care—would represent the frequently alleged irresponsibility of physicians who view their patients as curiosities and raw materials for science rather than as people to be healed. This reconceptualization of the collectivity-orientations of physicians, then, would serve as an additional dependent variable to be analyzed in terms of the basic typology. Surely scientists were primarily committed to the scholar-collectivity in their research activities, but did they carry over this commitment to patient-care situations?

The development and refinement of this conceptual scheme was one of the more exciting stages of the study. It took place at a time when I was particularly feeling the lack of a theoretical framework which I might suggest was being tested by the empirical study, thereby validating the "scientific" legitimacy of the study. As a result, I attempted to locate questionnaire items which might reasonably represent the new theoretical concepts. More hundreds of pages of computer output went into this attempt, and ultimately I was able to create indexes of universalism-particularism and specificity-diffuseness. The two indexes were related to one another as expected, but a careful validation of them indicated they measured quite different dimensions, as had been hoped.

Although this line of analysis seemed to hold a great deal of potential, it was limited from the very start by the data which were available from the survey. More important, however, I soon found myself grounded on the rocks of typological analysis, as had happened earlier. While it was fairly simple to treat the typology as an independent variable, differentially describing the attitudes of the four types, it was virtually impossible to discover the sources of the types, to treat the typology as a dependent variable. Since this was an important concern of the overall study, the limitation provided by the typology (rather than a unidimensional index) seriously threatened the ultimate worth of the analysis.

Finally, a very painful decision was made to discard the Parsonian exercise and return instead to the more straightforward analysis of faculty orientations to science. Perhaps the reader will sense the unhappiness of such a decision (and may have made one himself). After months of running tables, creating indexes, drafting new chapters, and changing the terminology of old ones, the enterprise was ultimately abandoned. Little if any of the reconceptualization is apparent in the present draft of the report. Yet as I reread the final text, I find myself casting it automatically within the framework which almost was: the one which didn't quite fit the data available this time around. For me, then, it provides a very definite, though implicit, theoretical substructure for the report.

Most researchers, I suspect, would be embarrassed to admit the rather late arrival of their theoretical model and its failure to fit with the data analyzed. I feel that such embarrassment is inappropriate. To my mind, this chain of events only emphasizes the close interaction between theory and empirical research in the social sciences, and in science generally, for that matter. The interaction is real, and no more so for one or even a hundred researchers having admitted it. Theories are not keenly and rigorously deduced in some tower of academic abstraction to be tested later by empirical studies. Facts themselves suggest theories, and theories then suggest other possible facts to be searched for in yet another turn of the cycle.[6]

One final observation may be in order to conclude this informal biography. The nonscientific reader may have formed the opinion that this purportedly scientific research was not as "scientific" as might otherwise have been imagined. There were so many false leads, so much inefficiency, so many chance stimuli. I can only comment that it was even more unsettling than the preceding pages have communicated. Seemingly important findings or interpretations would appear in a thunderclap, redirecting the entire thrust of the analysis, and a week later I would find I had essentially forgotten them. That which had seemed so very important one day would only be remembered or rediscovered by chance later—even though I had written perhaps ten or fifteen pages of rough draft about it. At other times, I would become very uneasy about a particular interpretation, feeling that either it was trivial, or it had

6. I do not pretend that this thesis is original with this writing. Among countless others, Robert K. Merton in *Social Theory and Social Structure* (New York: Free Press, 1967), chapters 2 and 3, and Phillip Hammond in *Sociologists at Work* have spoken candidly to this point. And yet the myth persists.

already been said, or it was simply unfounded. The preparation of the present manuscript was a collection of such episodes and very disconcerting. After weeks or even months of grappling with a particular problem, I would find myself back at the same conclusion or interpretation, feeling a fool for having wasted so much time.

Two things sustained me during this painful process. One was the discovery that my experience was not unique in science. Increasingly, I became aware of colleagues experiencing the same problems. More important, perhaps, I came across an excellent volume on Charles Darwin and evolution.[7] In that account of Darwin's struggles with data and ideas, I found the same uncertainties, wanderings, wasted time, and returns to old ideas that had been so disconcerting in my own work. Finally, I think I may have discovered what science is all about.

The second source of sustenance was the discovery of an ancient (Zen?) proverb: "The ignorant man says 'a mountain is a mountain.' The educated man says 'a mountain is more than just a mountain.' But the enlightened man says 'a mountain is a mountain.'" Whether I became enlightened in this process, I shall not venture to say. Yet with each wandering return to the old conclusion that the mountain was a mountain, there was the distinct feeling that I knew the mountain a little better.

7. William Irvine, *Apes, Angels, and Victorians* (New York: Meridian Books, 1959).

Sampling Design
and Verification

The original purpose of the sampling design in this study was to select a group of medical school faculty members who would represent all the full-time and part-time faculty members in the departments of Medicine and Pediatrics in the nation. This appendix describes the methods employed to that end and evaluates the representativeness of those faculty members who were selected and who participated in the study.

In brief overview, there are adequate grounds for concluding that the full-time faculty respondents provide a close representation of their counterparts across the nation. Only a small proportion of the part-time faculty sample responded to the questionnaire, however, and there are no adequate means available for testing the representativeness of those who did participate. As a result, the analysis in this report has been limited to the full-time faculty respondents; the part-time faculty sample will not be examined. For this reason, the discussion to follow is chiefly concerned with the full-time faculty members who participated in the study. The reader should bear in mind, however, that the original sampling design was intended to select adequate samples from both groups.

Identifying the Universe of Full-time Faculty Members

This book is intended as a description and analysis of a particular group of people: the full-time faculty members holding the ranks of professor, associate professor, assistant professor, or instructor in the departments of Medicine and Pediatrics in the nation's medical colleges. According to information provided by the Association of American Medical Colleges (AAMC), there were 2,532 such faculty members in Medicine and 1,162 in Pediatrics during the 1964–65 academic year.[1] These 3,694 faculty members, then, are the universe from which the present sample was selected.

While determining the number of full-time faculty members at any given time is relatively simple, learning *who* they are is another matter. There is no single list of their names; the only feasible access to this group is through the faculty rosters maintained by the several colleges employing them. The source most readily available is the roster of faculty published in the individual course catalogues. While such lists do not distinguish full-time from part-time faculty accurately, the lists were sufficient for the original study design which called for an examination of both groups.

The decision regarding the size of the sample to be designed was also based on the intention to study both full-time and part-time faculty. The size of the full-time universe could be determined with some accuracy, but the number of part-time faculty members in Medicine and Pediatrics had to be estimated from incomplete information. Ultimately, it was estimated that the combined universe of full-time and part-time faculty was approximately 12,000. A national sample of 2,000 faculty was judged sufficient for the project's purposes, and the decision was made, therefore, to design a procedure which would select a one-sixth sample.

1. This information is taken from a private communication with the AAMC.

Selection of the Medical School Sample

During the pilot study, it became evident that many medical school administrations were somewhat reluctant to participate in a survey of their faculty members. Selecting proportionate samples of faculty members from all the nation's medical schools, therefore, was judged a hopeless task, and the decision was made to employ a two-stage sampling design in which (a) a one-sixth sample of colleges would be selected with equal probability, and (b) all appropriate faculty members at each of the selected schools would be included in the study.

In view of the aims of the project, the universe of medical colleges was limited to those members of the AAMC which (a) offered a regular four-year medical curriculum, and (b) resided in the continental United States. To ensure against the possibility of selecting an unrepresentative sample of colleges, a procedure of stratification by size and geographical location was employed. First, the 84 colleges were grouped according to nine geographical regions.[2] Within each of the nine groups, schools were then arranged according to size. Next, the stratified list of medical colleges was numbered consecutively from 1 to 84. Since a one-sixth sample was desired, a random number was selected between 1 and 6. The school bearing this randomly selected number, and every sixth school following it in the list, constituted the sample of medical colleges. The 14 schools selected in this manner varied in both size and region.[3]

The medical colleges for the sample having been selected,

2. The nine geographical regions are New England, Middle Atlantic, East North Central, West North Central, South Atlantic, East South Central, West South Central, Mountain, and Pacific.
3. Throughout the project, faculty members and medical college administrators have been assured that the names of participating schools would be kept confidential. As a result, descriptions of the sample of schools has been presented in summary forms rather than in a list of the schools.

letters were sent to the respective deans, explaining the aims and methods of the project and asking permission to contact their faculty members. After several follow-up letters and telephone calls, nine of the fourteen schools agreed to participate. For the five who refused, replacements were selected from the stratified list. By the toss of a coin, one of the schools appearing next to the refusal was chosen as a replacement, thus insuring adequate representation by size and region. Of the five replacements, however, two refused to participate, forcing another administrative decision. Since the sample selection had already taken more time than was anticipated, the question arose as to whether the twelve schools willing to participate would provide an adequately representative sample. After a comparison of the 84 schools in the universe with the 12 selected schools, the decision was made to proceed with those who had agreed to par-

TABLE C-1

COMPARISON OF THE UNIVERSE AND
SAMPLE OF MEDICAL COLLEGES

	Universe (84 schools)	Sample (12 schools)
(a) Percentage distribution of schools by region:		
i. New England and Middle Atlantic....	26%	24%
ii. East North Central and West North Central..........................	26	25
iii. South Atlantic, East South Central, and West South Central..............	36	33
iv. Mountain and Pacific...............	12	17
(b) Average number of medical students........	377	428
(c) Average number of interns and residents....	213	196
(d) Average number of advanced students in the Basic Sciences (Masters, Doctoral, and Postdoctoral programs)....................	70	79
(e) Average number of Postdoctoral Clinical Fellows................................	50	64
(f) Ratio of line (d) above to line (e)..........	1.40	1.23

ticipate. Some of the comparisons underlying that decision are presented in table C-1.

An examination of the comparisons in table C-1 indicates that while the sample of 12 colleges is not, of course, a complete mirror-image of the universe of 84, there are no large nor consistent differences between the two. The regional distribution of the sample schools is nearly identical to the distribution of the 84 AAMC schools. The sample schools are only slightly larger than the national average, and the relative emphases on advanced training in basic science and clinical medicine are very similar.

Faculty Members' Response Rate

In terms of the original plan, the second stage of sampling involved contacting all the full-time and part-time instructors, assistant professors, associate professors, and professors in the departments of Medicine and Pediatrics at each of the selected schools. In a few cases, the college administrations provided up-to-date lists for this purpose; in most cases, the faculty lists contained in the college catalogues were used. This procedure generated a list of 2,491 faculty members (full-time and part-time), each of whom was sent a copy of the questionnaire reproduced in appendix D.

Throughout the planning of the project, it was agreed that participating faculty members ought to be guaranteed complete anonymity. To overcome the problems this created for control of the data-collection process, the following procedure was adopted. In addition to the questionnaire, faculty members received a postcard bearing their name, addressed to the project office. Each was asked to return the postcard upon completing his questionnaire. In this manner it was possible to guarantee anonymity, while at the same time maintaining a record of who had participated and who had not. At six-week intervals, those faculty members who had not returned their postcards were sent another copy of the questionnaire with a special appeal for participation. Two such follow-up mailings were undertaken.

It will be recalled that the faculty rosters available for sampling generally did not distinguish full-time and part-time faculty. Information provided by the AAMC, however, indicates there were 627 full-time faculty in the departments of Medicine and Pediatrics at the 12 selected colleges during the academic year considered in the project. If all 627 full-time faculty members had completed and returned their questionnaires, their responses might have been taken on face value as reasonably representative of their colleagues across the nation. Of, course, this seldom if ever happens. Yet, 454 full-time faculty members (72 per cent) did return completed questionnaires.[4] In comparison with other surveys of professions, and of medicine in particular, this return rate is very high.

In addition to the high return rate achieved among full-time faculty members, it is possible to test the representativeness of this group through two independent procedures. First, six weeks after the third wave of questionnaires had been sent, a one-third sample of the remaining nonrespondents (full-time and part-time) were sent a short postcard questionnaire. This final questionnaire was designed to collect basic background information on the nonrespondents which could point to any important differences between those who did and did not complete the primary questionnaire. At the same time, however, it was necessary to design a questionnaire which would be short and simple to complete—one which might be completed by those faculty members who were either unable or unwilling to take the time necessary to complete the primary questionnaire.

Since a one-third sample of all nonrespondents was selected

4. This determination is based on respondents' own reporting in the questionnaire of their status.
5. The distribution of the universe has been computed from the data provided by the AAMC in a private correspondence.

for this final questionnaire, it is reasonable to assume that approximately one-third (about 58) of the full-time faculty non-respondents were selected. Virtually all (52) replied. Table C-2, then, is a test of the assumption that full-time faculty members who completed the survey questionnaire do not differ significantly from those who did not complete the questionnaire.

TABLE C-2

COMPARISON OF FULL-TIME FACULTY RESPONDENTS
AND NONRESPONDENTS

	Respondents* 100% = (454)	Nonrespondents† (52)
(a) Sex:		
Male....................	92%	90%
Female.................	8 ·	10
(b) Age:		
Under 35...............	26%	20%
36–45.................	47	53
46–55.................	21	22
56–65.................	4	6
Over 65................	2	0
(c) Academic rank:		
Instructor..............	15%	13%
Assistant professor.........	36	42
Associate professor.........	25	21
Professor..............	24	23
(d) When M.D. degree was received:		
1920 to 1929..............	2%	0%
1930 to 1939..............	8	8
1940 to 1949..............	32	33
1950 to 1959..............	52	56
1960 to 1964..............	6	4

* Based on the information provided by the 454 full-time faculty members who completed and returned the main survey questionnaires.
† Based on the information provided by the 52 full-time faculty members who did not complete the main survey questionnaires, but who completed the short postcard questionnaires.

Again, we note that the two groups are not identical, but the differences which are evident are neither large enough nor consistent enough to be significant. In other words, the 28 percent of the full-time faculty who did not participate in the study do not seem significantly different from those who did. Hence, there are sufficient grounds for assuming that the responses given by the 454 participants will adequately mirror the responses that would have been received if all 627 full-time faculty members had participated.

The second attempt at verification of the full-time sample is aimed at determining how closely the 454 participants represent the larger national group. Table C-3 presents the comparison of the full-time universe and the respondents with regard to academic rank and department.

TABLE C-3

PROPORTIONATE DISTRIBUTIONS OF UNIVERSE AND SAMPLE
BY DEPARTMENT AND ACADEMIC RANK
(FULL-TIME FACULTY)

		Academic Rank		
	Instructor	Assistant Professor	Associate Professor	Professor
Distribution of Universe				
Medicine	.1426	.2208	.1775	.1442
Pediatrics	.0714	.1107	.0722	.0600
Distribution of Respondents				
Medicine	.1151	.2685	.1798	.1798
Pediatrics	.1335	.0863	.0719	.0647

Except for slight variations, the overall distribution of respondents in the survey closely matches the distribution of full-time faculty members whom they are to represent. This final test of representativeness only confirms the previous observations in the appendix. The twelve schools selected for the study seem representative of the 84 member schools in the AAMC (table C-1), the full-time faculty who replied to the survey closely resemble those who did not reply (table C-2), and, finally, the distribution of the 454 full-time faculty members participating in the study provides a close approximation of the distribution of the universe of full-time faculty members in the two departments nationally.

Part-time Faculty Response

Only 313 (17 percent) of the part-time faculty members selected in the sample completed and returned their questionnaires. To a large extent this seems to reflect the necessity of contacting all faculty members through the medical schools where they were employed, and there are some suggestions that many of the part-time faculty did not receive the materials sent to them. It is also possible that part-time faculty members were less likely to feel that a study of medical education was directly relevant to them than was the case for full-time faculty, although there is no way of testing this.

In addition to the low rate of return among part-time faculty members, there is a lack of national records for testing the overall representativeness of those who did participate. It is for these reasons that the present report has not examined the part-time faculty sample.

Summary

The foregoing discussion has revolved primarily around the question of analytic description. If 60 percent of the full-time faculty members in the sample say yes in response to a particular question, we shall be safe in assuming that roughly the same proportion of full-time university internists and pediatricians in the nation would give the same answer. In most of the analysis, however, we are more interested in explanation than in simple description. That is, we not only wish to know how many would say yes but also *why* they say yes while others say no. In an explanatory analysis such as this, the absolute representativeness of the sample is somewhat less critical than would be the case for a descriptive analysis. The 454 full-time faculty members are clearly sufficient for our explanatory purposes.

APPENDIX D

Questionnaire

UNIVERSITY OF CALIFORNIA
SAN FRANCISCO MEDICAL CENTER

SCHOOL OF MEDICINE
DEPARTMENT OF MEDICINE

OCTOBER, 1965

DEAR COLLEAGUE:

This booklet contains a questionnaire which I feel will be of interest to you as medical educator, scientist and physician, and which I hope you will be good enough to answer.

Although there has been a continuing discussion for years on the varieties of professional activities and attitudes of medical school faculty members, there is hardly any empirical information available on the implicit philosophies which underlie medicine and medical education. Informative as current surveys are concerning medical education as *education,* we are afforded only the most general observations about the unique aspects of *medical* education. While the present study espouses no one philosophical position, it is my hope that it will provide an empirical baseline of existing orientations to aid in the critical dialogue regarding the goals of medical education. For, consciously or unconsciously, our actions and attitudes mirror our most basic philosophies.

This questionnaire represents the final stage of a national survey of medical school faculty members in the departments of Medicine and Pediatrics. It is being conducted under a grant from the National Institutes of Health and with the consent of the Association of American Medical Colleges and the dean of your medical school. The Survey Research Center at the University of California, Berkeley, is cooperating with the project and some questions reflect problems of sociological interest. During the past two years, we have contacted faculty members at seven medical schools in pilot-tests designed to evaluate and refine our research instrument. This mailing represents the culmination of that effort, and I hope you will assist the project by granting us approximately 20 to 30 minutes required to complete the questionnaire. The fourteen medical schools participating in this final survey differ widely in size as well as geographical location. Together they constitute a representative sample of faculty members in Medicine and Pediatrics across the United States. Therefore, it is important that everyone contacted participate.

You will notice that two copies of the questionnaire have been included. Please complete *one* of them and return it to us. No envelope or postage is required; simply fold over the back cover and seal. The second questionnaire is for your own files. The postcard which has been included should be mailed at the same time the questionnaire is completed and sent to us. Since the questionnaire itself is anonymous (the number stamped on it simply identifies your school), the card is to let us know your questionnaire has been returned. And since I should like to send copies of the summarized findings of the study to those who participate, the postcards also will provide a mailing list for that purpose.

As a member of the medical school faculty at the University of California in San Francisco, let me assure you I am painfully aware of the flood of questionnaires which fills our mailboxes. Knowing this, I would have never suggested such a study if I did not sincerely believe the information we shall gain is crucial to recognizing basic requirements of current and future medical education, and cannot be obtained in any other way.

Thanking you for any courtesy you may be able to extend us in this matter, I remain,

Very sincerely yours,

Otto E. Guttentag, M.D. (s)
*Samuel Hahnemann Professor
of Medical Philosophy*

To Mail: No envelope or postage is required for returning this questionnaire.

THE TEACHING PHYSICIAN

Instructions

Either pen or pencil may be used to complete the questionnaire.
Please disregard the small numbers and letters next to each question; these are for
the use of IBM tabulating machine operators.

In the first section, we would like to learn something about your interests and
opinions regarding a number of issues which concern the medical profession in
general and medical schools in particular.

Part I. PROFESSIONAL INTERESTS AND OPINIONS

1. While some medical students find it more natural to view each patient as an
   individual person, others are more likely to perceive him as an example of a
   disease entity. Do you feel the overall medical school experience at the school
   where you teach has any effect on the way students ultimately view patients
   in this regard?

   $^{8}/_{A}$ ☐ Yes, it creates a shift toward viewing the patient as an individual person.

   B ☐ Yes, it creates a shift toward viewing the patient as an example of a disease
   entity.

   C ☐ No, there seems to be no effect.

2. Do you feel medical school training *should* encourage either or both of these
   views, or do you feel the issue is irrelevant to medical training?

   $^{9}/_{A}$ ☐ It should encourage a view of the patient as an individual person.

   B ☐ It should encourage a view of the patient as an example of a disease entity.

   C ☐ It should encourage both views equally.

   D ☐ The issue is irrelevant to medical training.

3. When students have their first prolonged contacts with particular patients, do
   you feel there is generally a greater tendency for them to become overly involved with their patients, or a greater tendency to remain overly detached?

   $^{10}/_{A}$ ☐ There is a greater tendency to become overly involved.

   B ☐ There is a greater tendency to remain overly detached.

   C ☐ Both seem to occur about equally.

1

4. If you were responsible for supervising a student in the prolonged care of a particular patient, would you rather see the student become somewhat too involved in his patient, or remain somewhat too detached?

$^{11}/_A$ ☐ Become somewhat too involved

 $_B$ ☐ Remain somewhat too detached

5. The medical student's first introduction to the cadaver is generally regarded as a major step in his professional training. Below, we have summarized what seem to be two common, though quite different, approaches to this stage of training. Which statement comes closest to expressing your own feelings?

$^{12}/_A$ ☐ Students should be reminded of the special privilege of working on a human body, lest they lose sight of the basic humanity of the medical profession.

 $_B$ ☐ Students should be encouraged to view the cadaver as a complex laboratory specimen, thus maintaining scientific detachment in understanding its structure and function.

6. It is generally recognized that some medical duties require considerable understanding by the physician of the personal problems of his patients' lives while other duties call for a definitely detached attitude. Generally speaking, which of these orientations is the more appropriate to the type of patient contacts which occur in connection with most of your present faculty duties?

$^{13}/_A$ ☐ Personal involvement is definitely more appropriate.

 $_B$ ☐ Personal involvement is probably more appropriate.

 $_C$ ☐ Personal detachment is probably more appropriate.

 $_D$ ☐ Personal detachment is definitely more appropriate.

7. As a medical school faculty member, in what capacity do you feel you can make your greatest *teaching* contribution: as a practicing physician or as a medical researcher?

$^{14}/_A$ ☐ Practicing physician

 $_B$ ☐ Medical researcher

8. If you could plan the pattern of your duties as a medical school instructor, which *one* of the following do you feel would be the most enjoyable for you?

$^{15}/_A$ ☐ Caring for patients and researching those problems which were involved in their care

 $_B$ ☐ Caring for patients and using particular patients to illustrate pathological processes to students

 $_C$ ☐ Supervising students and house staff in the care of patients

2

D ☐ Doing basic research in clinical medicine

E ☐ Doing research in total patient symptomatology and developing better diagnostic techniques and treatments

9. When you function as a physician, would you generally *prefer* serving as an attending physician or as a consultant? (Please disregard the factor of financial reimbursement and the nature of your present duties.)

16/A ☐ Attending physician

B ☐ Consultant

10. As you continue to advance your own medical knowledge, would you say your ultimate medical interests lie primarily in the direction of total patient management, or the understanding of basic mechanisms?

17/A ☐ Total patient management

B ☐ Basic mechanisms

11. Generally speaking, how would you rate the overall quality of students at your school who go into *academic* medical careers, compared with the rest of their classmates?

18/A ☐ Well above average

B ☐ Slightly above average

C ☐ About average

D ☐ Slightly below average

E ☐ Well below average

    11a. How would you rate those who go into careers in *general practice?*

       19/A ☐ Well above average

       B ☐ Slightly above average

       C ☐ About average

       D ☐ Slightly below average

       E ☐ Well below average

    11b. How would you rate those who go into careers in *specialized practice?*

       20/A ☐ Well above average

       B ☐ Slightly above average

       C ☐ About average

       D ☐ Slightly below average

       E ☐ Well below average

12. Do you feel that the general caliber of students entering *any* of these careers presents a problem serious enough to warrant some program whereby medical schools would actively encourage a larger proportion of the best students to

3

choose such careers? Please place a check mark beside each career in which you feel a sufficiently serious problem exists.

$^{21}/_A$ ☐ Academic medical careers

$^{22}/_A$ ☐ General practice

$^{23}/_A$ ☐ Specialized practice

$^{24}/_A$ ☐ None

13. From what you may have heard or read about the Comprehensive Care programs instituted by some medical schools in recent years, do you generally approve or disapprove of the general purpose of these programs?

$^{25}/_A$ ☐ Strongly approve

　B ☐ Somewhat approve

　C ☐ Somewhat disapprove

　D ☐ Strongly disapprove

　E ☐ I have not formed an opinion

14. Recently, the American Academy of General Practitioners declared the role of Family Physician a medical specialty. Generally speaking, did you approve or disapprove of that decision?

$^{26}/_A$ ☐ Strongly approved

　B ☐ Approved somewhat

　C ☐ Disapproved somewhat

　D ☐ Strongly disapproved

　E ☐ I had no opinion on the decision

15. Several medical colleges have begun consideration of "family care" programs aimed specifically at training family physicians. If such a program were being considered for the university where you teach, which of the following statements do you feel would come closest to your own reaction?

$^{27}/_A$ ☐ Would oppose such a program altogether

　B ☐ Would favor my school collaborating with a non-university general hospital which would be willing to run such a program

　C ☐ Would favor such a program at my school in which at least the key members of the program would have full-time faculty status

16. Everyone knows that university hospitals have the most modern scientific equipment which is available, but it has been observed that patients react to this differently. From your own observations, please indicate how common each of the following reactions seems to be among the patients treated at your hospital.

4

	Very Common	Fairly Common	Fairly Uncommon	Very Uncommon

a. The patient feels threatened by the prospect of being a guinea pig .... ^{28}/A ☐ B ☐ C ☐ D ☐

b. The patient realizes that he will receive the best medical treatment in a university hospital .... ^{29}/A ☐ B ☐ C ☐ D ☐

c. The patient feels he is just a number in a cold atmosphere .... ^{30}/A ☐ B ☐ C ☐ D ☐

17. In a community which has both a university hospital and non-university, general hospitals, do you feel the university hospital should be reserved for referrals exclusively, or do you feel general hospital facilities should be provided there also?

^{31}/A ☐ Referrals exclusively

B ☐ General hospital facilities also

18. In the field of therapeutic research, are you generally more interested in articles reporting evaluations of the effectiveness of various treatments or articles exploring the basic rationale underlying the treatments?

^{32}/A ☐ Primarily articles evaluating effectiveness

B ☐ Both types, but somewhat more interested in articles evaluating effectiveness

C ☐ Both types, but somewhat more interested in articles exploring basic rationale

D ☐ Primarily articles exploring basic rationale

19. Suppose the following lectures were offered in your hospital:

(a) In your opinion, which 2 lectures would bring out the largest audience among the staff at your hospital?

(b) Which 2 would interest you most?

	(a) Largest audience (Check 2)	(b) Greatest personal interest (Check 2)
"Group Practice—Pros and Cons"	$^{33\text{-}34}$/A ☐	$^{35\text{-}36}$/A ☐
"Office Treatment of Thyroid Disorders"	B ☐	B ☐
"Lipid Metabolism"	C ☐	C ☐
"How to Avoid Malpractice Suits"	D ☐	D ☐
"Stimulants and Sedatives"	E ☐	E ☐
"The Role of Serotonin in Disorders of the Gut" ..	F ☐	F ☐

5

20. Which of the following would you consider the best practical training for a *full-time* faculty member in your department?

   37/A ☐ Experience as a family physician

   B ☐ Experience as a specialized practitioner

   C ☐ Experience as a medical scientist

   D ☐ Experience as a basic science investigator

21. Here is a somewhat different type of question. It is evident from current literature that some researchers are considering the modification of genetic endowment (c.f. "genetic surgery," "germinal choice" and the induction of parthenogenetic development) in terms of controlling human evolution. The prospect of such applications of this research has aroused diverse reactions. Some of the frequently heard comments are listed below; beside each, please indicate whether you strongly agree (SA), agree (A), disagree (D), strongly disagree (SD), or whether you are undecided (U).

	SA	A	D	SD	U
a. The potential social dangers of such research place it outside the legitimate realm of medical science ....38/A ☐		B ☐	C ☐	D ☐	E ☐
b. Before such research continues, the scientific community must resolve a number of moral and ethical questions regarding its possible consequences ....39/A ☐		B ☐	C ☐	D ☐	E ☐
c. The applications of such research should be restricted by some agency of the larger society ....40/A ☐		B ☐	C ☐	D ☐	E ☐
d. This whole topic has generated more discussion and speculation than it really warrants ....14/A ☐		B ☐	C ☐	D ☐	E ☐

22. Suppose you were the attending physician for a non-private ward patient who had died. Would you personally speak to the surviving family, or would you delegate this duty to the house staff?

   42/A ☐ In almost every instance, I would speak to them personally

   B ☐ As a general rule, I would speak to them personally, although I might occasionally delegate this duty to the house staff

   C ☐ As a general rule, I would delegate this duty to the house staff, although I might occasionally speak to the surviving family personally

   D ☐ In almost every instance, I would delegate this duty to the house staff

6

23. In the development of medical science, if it is deemed necessary to subject a group of healthy volunteers to a potentially dangerous experiment, do you feel the experimenter himself should or should not participate as an experimental subject? (Assume he is a suitable experimental subject.)

⁴³/ₐ ☐ I feel he has a *moral obligation* to participate
   ᴮ ☐ I feel it is *generally unwise* for him to participate
   ᴄ ☐ I feel he should be *prohibited* from participating
   ᴅ ☐ Other (Please specify)

----

24. During the recent thalidomide alarm, many prospective mothers reportedly asked their physicians to allow their babies to die at birth if any bizarre deformities were present. If a physician had complied with such a request and was being tried for murder, do you think you would be sympathetic to his case or not?

⁴⁴/ₐ ☐ Definitely sympathetic   ᴄ ☐ Probably not sympathetic
   ᴮ ☐ Probably sympathetic   ᴅ ☐ Definitely not sympathetic

25. The single most controversial social issue in medical circles this last year has been that of Medical Care for the Aged (Medicare). As you understand this program, what is your overall opinion of it?

⁴⁵/ₐ ☐ Strongly approve   ᴄ ☐ Disapprove somewhat
   ᴮ ☐ Approve somewhat   ᴅ ☐ Strongly disapprove

26. Finally, here is a series of statements, some of which deal with medicine and medical education, and some which deal with sociological problems. While you may feel some of the statements are too complex for the requested answers, nevertheless, decisions on these types of questions have proven helpful in sharpening outlines of professional orientations. Please indicate whether you are most inclined to strongly agree (SA), agree (A), disagree (D), strongly disagree (SD), or whether you are undecided (U) about each of the statements.

	SA	A	D	SD	U
a. Every physician should have been hospitalized as a patient at some time .....⁴⁶/ₐ	☐	ᴮ ☐	ᴄ ☐	ᴅ ☐	ᴇ ☐
b. There is a tendency these days for medical research to wander too far away from actual problems of preventing and curing disease ....⁴⁷/ₐ	☐	ᴮ ☐	ᴄ ☐	ᴅ ☐	ᴇ ☐

7

	SA	A	D	SD	U

c. The greatest advances in the history of
medicine have been made by physicians
faced with practical medical problems ....⁴⁸/A ☐   B ☐   C ☐   D ☐   E ☐

d. Most people on welfare could take care of
themselves if they really wanted to ....⁴⁹/A ☐   B ☐   C ☐   D ☐   E ☐

e. Willpower is the essential force for
overcoming social difficulties ....⁵⁰/A ☐   B ☐   C ☐   D ☐   E ☐

Parts II–VI of this questionnaire are designed to ascertain the nature and extent of your involvement in the several professional roles of a medical school faculty member—those of teacher, research scientist and physician. To determine the interplay among these various roles, we have asked you to report briefly on the academic year, 1964–65.

Part II.   RESEARCH ACTIVITIES

27. Have you ever been actively engaged in research during any period in your medical career?

⁵¹/A ☐ Yes

B ☐ No (Please skip to question #32)

28. During the 1964–65 academic year, were you actively engaged in research?

⁵²/A ☐ Yes

B ☐ No

29. In what area(s) do your research interests lie? (Please check as many as apply and add any area not listed in which you have a research interest.)

⁵³/A ☐ Subcellular processes (e.g., enzyme, metabolic chemistry)

⁵⁴/B ☐ Cellular processes (cellular physiology; e.g., membrane properties, tissue culture)

⁵⁵/C ☐ Organ and organ system processes (organ and organ system physiology and metabolism including pathophysiologic states)

⁵⁶/D ☐ Epidemiology (ecology)

⁵⁷/E ☐ Psychosomatic medicine

⁵⁸/F ☐ Medical education

⁵⁹/G ☐ Study of patients' total symptomatology and course of disease (disease entity) with or without treatment

8

$^{60}/_\text{H}$ ☐ Child development

$^{61}/_\text{I}$ ☐ Comprehensive child supervision

$^{62}/_\text{A}$ ☐ Other(s) (Please specify)..

....

....

30. If you have checked more than one area in question #29, please encircle the check mark beside the area of your *primary* interest.
$63/$

31. Does your research require your personal contact with patients? (Check the *one* answer which best applies.)

$^{64}/_\text{A}$ ☐ No, it requires no contact with patients

  $_\text{B}$ ☐ Yes, primarily in order to perform a special technique (e.g., liver biopsy)

  $_\text{C}$ ☐ Yes, primarily in order to take a comprehensive history and/or to perform an extensive physical examination

  $_\text{D}$ ☐ Yes, other (Please specify)..

....

Part III.   TEACHING DUTIES

32. During the 1964–65 academic year, approximately what proportion of the *1st year students* did you instruct?

$^{65}/_\text{A}$ ☐ None

  $_\text{B}$ ☐ Less than one-fourth of the class

  $_\text{C}$ ☐ One-fourth to one-half of the class

  $_\text{D}$ ☐ More than one-half of the class

33. Now would you please answer the same question with regard to the second, third, and fourth year students and for the house staff by placing a check mark in the appropriate space in *each* of the columns below?

	Second Year	Third Year	Fourth Year	House Staff
None	$^{66}/_\text{A}$ ☐	$^{67}/_\text{A}$ ☐	$^{68}/_\text{A}$ ☐	$^{69}/_\text{A}$ ☐
Less than one-fourth	$_\text{B}$ ☐	$_\text{B}$ ☐	$_\text{B}$ ☐	$_\text{B}$ ☐
One-fourth to one-half	$_\text{C}$ ☐	$_\text{C}$ ☐	$_\text{C}$ ☐	$_\text{C}$ ☐
More than one-half	$_\text{D}$ ☐	$_\text{D}$ ☐	$_\text{D}$ ☐	$_\text{D}$ ☐

9

34. During the 1964–65 academic year, approximately how many hours per week, on the average, did you devote to the following types of teaching situations?

For each type of teaching situation, please place a check mark in the column representing the appropriate number of *hours per week*.

	None	Less than 5	5–10	More than 10
Lecture presentations	70/A ☐	B ☐	C ☐	D ☐
Seminars	71/A ☐	B ☐	C ☐	D ☐
Laboratory instruction	72/A ☐	B ☐	C ☐	D ☐
Preceptor-type instruction (e.g., ward rounds, tutorial sessions, informal conferences, etc.)	73/A ☐	B ☐	C ☐	D ☐

35. What courses, if any, were you ultimately responsible for during the 1964–65 academic year? Please list the course titles.

74/

Part IV. OUTPATIENT DEPARTMENT PRACTICE

36. During the 1964–65 academic year, how many months (total), if any, were you assigned to the outpatient department?

S/A ☐ None (Please skip to question #40)

B ☐ Less than one month

C ☐ One to three months

D ☐ Three to six months

E ☐ Six to nine months

F ☐ Nine to twelve months

37. Below is a series of questions relating to the various capacities in which you might have served during your assignment to the outpatient department. Please indicate whether you served in each of those capacities.

a. Did you serve directly as the attending physician, *including* the responsibility for making emergency calls on behalf of the patients assigned to your care?

9/A ☐ Regularly   B ☐ Sometimes   C ☐ Never

10

b. Did you serve directly as the attending physician, *excluding* the responsibility for making emergency calls on behalf of the patients assigned to your care?

¹⁰/_A ☐ Regularly   _B ☐ Sometimes   _C ☐ Never

c. Did you serve as house staff consultant:

    i. for total patient management?

    ¹¹/_A ☐ Regularly   _B ☐ Sometimes   _C ☐ Never

    ii. for specific disorders?

    ¹²/_A ☐ Regularly   _B ☐ Sometimes   _C ☐ Never

d. Did you serve as consultant to students:

    i. for total patient management?

    ¹³/_A ☐ Regularly   _B ☐ Sometimes   _C ☐ Never

    ii. for specific disorders?

    ¹³/_A ☐ Regularly   _B ☐ Sometimes   _C ☐ Never

38. Was the clinic in which you received most of your outpatient department patients a departmental clinic, an interdepartmental clinic, or one which was associated with a particular institute?

¹⁵/_A ☐ Departmental clinic

    _B ☐ Interdepartmental clinic

    _C ☐ Clinic associated with an institute

39. What is the specific name of that clinic? (e.g., General Medicine, General Pediatrics, or sub-specialty clinic designation)

¹⁶/ --

Part V. HOSPITAL NON-PRIVATE PRACTICE

40. During the 1964–65 academic year, did you have an assignment as an *attending physician* on a non-private ward service, either on a continuing or a rotating basis?

¹⁷/_A ☐ Yes, on a continuing basis

    _B ☐ Yes, on a rotating basis

    _C ☐ No (Please skip to question #44)

41. During the 1964–65 academic year, how many months did you serve in that capacity; during that entire period, what was the approximate total number of staff patients assigned to your care (as attending physician on a non-private ward service)?

¹⁸⁻¹⁹/ ....Months   ²⁰/ ....Patients

11

42. What was the procedure by which the house staff reported to you on the care of the staff patients assigned to you as attending physician?

21/A ☐ House staff reported daily at a specified time

B ☐ House staff reported informally nearly every day

C ☐ House staff reported only when particular circumstances required your attention

D ☐ Other (Please specify)..

....

43. During your "off-duty" hours, what was the *normal* procedure for making major diagnostic and therapeutic decisions regarding the staff patients assigned to you as attending physician?

22/A ☐ Members of the house staff made these decisions

B ☐ "On-duty" faculty members made these decisions

C ☐ I was called to make these decisions.

D ☐ Other (Please specify)..

....

44. During the 1964–65 academic year, did you see non-private ward patients as a consultant?

23/A ☐ Yes

B ☐ No

Part VI.   PRIVATE PRACTICE

45. On the average, approximately how many private patients *per week* did you see during the 1964–65 academic year?

24/A ☐ None (Please skip to question #49)

B ☐ Less than five per week

C ☐ Six to ten per week

D ☐ Eleven to twenty-five per week

E ☐ More than twenty-five per week

46. Did you see your private patients primarily in your office or primarily in the hospital?

25/A ☐ Primarily in my office

B ☐ Primarily in the hospital

C ☐ Both about equally

12

47. In your private practice during the 1964–65 academic year, did you serve primarily as the attending physician or as a consultant?

$^{26}/_A$ ☐ Primarily as the attending physician

 $_B$ ☐ Primarily as a consultant

 $_C$ ☐ Both about equally

48. If you served as a consultant to private patients at all during the 1964–65 academic year, was this primarily in relation to total patient management or in relation to specific disorders?

$^{27}/_A$ ☐ Primarily in relation to total patient management

 $_B$ ☐ Primarily in relation to specific disorders

 $_C$ ☐ Both about equally

 $_D$ ☐ Did not serve as a consultant to private patients

In this section, we hope to learn something about your professional training to gain an insight into the sources and training of medical school faculty members.

Part VII. PROFESSIONAL BACKGROUND

49. From what medical school did you obtain your M.D. degree, and in what year?

School... Year..............

28-30/   31-32/

50. How many years have you held an appointment at your present school?............

33-34/

51. What is your present academic rank?

$^{35}/_A$ ☐ Instructor

 $_B$ ☐ Assistant Professor

 $_C$ ☐ Associate Professor

 $_D$ ☐ Professor

 $_E$ ☐ Other (Please specify)...

52. Is your faculty appointment full-time or part-time?

$^{36}/_A$ ☐ Full-time

 $_B$ ☐ Part-time

53. What is your department? $^{37}/$...

54. What is your board certification, if any? $^{38}/$...

55. What do you consider your specialty and/or sub-specialty, if any?

$^{39}/$ ....

13

56. Which single professional organization concerned with medical problems comes closest to reflecting your own field interest?

40/ ....

57. Have you ever been hospitalized as a patient, either before or after becoming a physician?

41/A ☐ Yes, before becoming a physician

  B ☐ Yes, after becoming a physician

  C ☐ Yes, both before and after becoming a physician

  D ☐ No, never hospitalized as a patient

Finally, we would like to ask you a few questions about your background. This information will help us to learn about the kinds of people who join medical school faculties. If you feel that any question is too personal, then please feel free to skip over it. However, all questionnaires will be completely anonymous and since this section is very important to the study, we hope you will answer each question.

Part VIII. PERSONAL BACKGROUND

58. Sex: 42/A ☐ Male   B ☐ Female

59. Marital status:

43/A ☐ Single

  B ☐ Married

  C ☐ Separated, widowed or divorced

60. Age:

44/A ☐ 35 or under

  B ☐ 36–45

  C ☐ 46–55

  D ☐ 56–65

  E ☐ Over 65

61. In what part of the country did you grow up? (Please check one.)

45/A ☐ The East

  B ☐ The South

  C ☐ The Midwest

  D ☐ The West

  E ☐ Other (Please specify)...

14

62. What was the size of the community in which you lived *most* of the time prior to entering college? (Please,check one.)

⁴⁶/ₐ ☐ Small farming community
ᴮ ☐ Less than 10,000 population (not a suburb)
ᴄ ☐ 10,000 to 25,000 population (not a suburb)
ᴅ ☐ 25,000 to 100,000 population (not a suburb)
ᴇ ☐ 100,000 to 250,000 population (not a suburb)
ꜰ ☐ 250,000 to 500,000 population (not a suburb)
ɢ ☐ 500,000 to one million population
ʜ ☐ Over one million population
ɪ ☐ Suburb of a city with less than 500,000 population
ᴊ ☐ Suburb of a city with more than 500,000 population

63. In what country was each of your parents born?
Mother ⁴⁷/... Father ⁴⁸/...

64. What is (was) your father's occupation? ⁴⁹/...

65. How do you tend to think of yourself politically?

⁵⁰/ₐ ☐ Very conservative
ᴮ ☐ Moderately conservative
ᴄ ☐ Moderately liberal
ᴅ ☐ Very liberal
ᴇ ☐ Other (Please specify)...

66. What is your religious preference?

⁵¹/ₐ ☐ Catholic
ᴮ ☐ Protestant (Denomination) ⁵²/...
ᴄ ☐ Jewish
ᴅ ☐ None
ᴇ ☐ Other (Please specify)...

67. In general, how important would you say your religion is to you?

⁵³/ₐ ☐ Extremely important
ᴮ ☐ Fairly important
ᴄ ☐ Fairly unimportant
ᴅ ☐ Not at all important

15

Thank you for your time and consideration in completing this questionnaire. If there are any further comments you would care to make in regard to this study or any of the issues covered in the questionnaire, the remaining space has been provided for that purpose and we welcome your remarks.

Selected
Sociomedical
Bibliographies

William Caudill, "Applied Anthropology in Medicine," *Anthropology Today*, A. L. Kroeber, ed. University of Chicago Press, 1953, 177–806.

Howard E. Freeman and Leo G. Reeder, "Medical Sociology: A Review of the Literature." *American Sociological Review 22* (1957): 73–81.

Oswald Hall, "Sociological Research in the Field of Medicine: Progress and Prospects." *American Sociological Review 16* (1951): 639–643.

A. R. Mangus, "Medical Sociology." *American Sociological Review 39* (1955): 158–164.

David Mechanic, *Medical Sociology: A Selective View*. New York: Free Press, 1968. 455–484.

Robert K. Merton, Samuel Bloom, and Natalie Rogoff, "Studies in the Sociology of Medical Education." *Journal of Medical Education 31* (1956): 552–564.

Marion Pearsall, *Medical Behavioral Science: A Selected Bibliography of Cultural Anthropology, Social Psychology and Sociology in Medicine*. Lexington: University of Kentucky Press, 1963.

George G. Reader and Mary E. W. Goss, "Medical Sociology with

Particular Reference to the Study of Hospitals." *Transactions of the Fourth World Congress of Sociology 2* (1959): 139–152.

George G. Reader and Mary E. W. Goss, "The Sociology of Medicine," *Sociology Today,* Robert K. Merton, Leonard Broom, and Leonard S. Cottrell, Jr., eds. New York: Basic Books, 1959. 229–246.

George Rosen and Edward Wellin, "A Bookshelf on the Social Sciences and Public Health." *American Journal of Public Health 49* (1959): 441–454.

W. Richard Scott and Edmund H. Volkart, eds., *Medical Care: Readings in the Sociology of Medical Institutions.* New York: John Wiley and Sons, 1966. (Several annotated bibliographies are provided throughout the book.)

Leo W. Simmons and Harold G. Wolff, *Social Science in Medicine.* New York: Russell Sage Foundation, 1954. 201–246.

Ozzie Simmons, "Social Research in Health and Medicine: A Bibliography," *Handbook of Medical Sociology,* Howard E. Freeman, Sol Levine, and Leo G. Reder, eds. Englewood Cliffs, N.J.: Prentice-Hall, 1963. 213–239.

Robert Straus, "The Nature and Status of Medical Sociology." *American Sociological Review 22* (1957): 200–204.

Index